Managing
EDUCATIONAL
DEVELOPMENT
PROJECTS

The Staff and Educational Development Series
Series Editor: James Wisdom

SEDA is the Staff and Education Development Association. It supports and encourages developments in teaching and learning in higher education through a variety of methods: publications, conferences, networking, journals, regional meetings and research – and through various SEDA Accreditation Schemes.

SEDA
Selly Wick House
59–61 Selly Wick Road
Selly Park
Birmingham B29 7JE
Tel: 0121 415 6801
Fax: 0121 415 6802
E-mail: office@seda.ac.uk

Managing
EDUCATIONAL DEVELOPMENT PROJECTS

Effective Management for Maximum Impact

Edited by
Carole Baume, Paul Martin & Mantz Yorke

SEDA
STAFF AND EDUCATIONAL
DEVELOPMENT ASSOCIATION

KOGAN
PAGE

First published in 2002

Kogan Page Limited
120 Pentonville Road
London N1 9JN
UK

Stylus Publishing Inc.
22883 Quicksilver Drive
Sterling VA 20166–2012
USA

British Library Cataloguing in Publication Data

A CIP record for this book is available from the British Library.

ISBN 0 7494 3882 7 (paperback)
ISBN 0 7494 3904 1 (hardback)

Typeset by Saxon Graphics Ltd, Derby
Printed and bound in Great Britain by Creative Print and Design (Wales) Ebbw Vale

Contents

Contributors

June Balshaw is leader of the Combined Studies Programme in the School of Humanities at the University of Greenwich
Address: Old Royal Naval College, Park Row, London SE10 9LS
E-mail: j.m.balshaw@gre.ac.uk

Carole Baume is Regional Director of the Open University in the North West
Address: 351 Altrincham Road, Sharston, Manchester M22 4UN
E-mail: c.baume@open.ac.uk

David Baume is a Higher Education Consultant
Address: 607 The Place, Ducie Street, Manchester M1 2TP
E-mail: ADBaume@aol.com

Sally Fincher is Lecturer in Computer Science at the University of Kent at Canterbury
Address: Computing Laboratory, Canterbury, Kent CT2 7NF
E-mail: s.a.fincher@ukc.ac.uk

Phil Gravestock is Project Manager of the Geography Discipline Network, Geography and Environmental Management Research Unit (GEMRU), University of Gloucestershire
Address: Francis Close Hall, Swindon Road, Cheltenham GL50 4AZ
E-mail: PGravestock@glos.ac.uk

Richard Johnstone is Pro-Vice-Chancellor at the University of Technology, Sydney
Address: PO Box 123, Broadway, NSW 2007, Australia
E-mail: richard.johnstone@uts.edu.au

Paul Martin is National Coordinator for the Teaching Quality Enhancement Fund
Address: Centre for Higher Education Practice, Open University, Walton Hall, Milton Keynes MK7 6AA
E-mail: p.r.martin@open.ac.uk

Howard Senter is a Distance Learning Consultant
Address: 31 Village Road, Cockayne Hatley, Sandy, Beds SG19 2EE
E-mail: CockHatley@aol.com

Angela Smallwood is Senior Lecturer in English Studies and Director of
the PADSHE Project at the University of Nottingham
Address: Centre for Teaching Enhancement, Jubilee Campus, Nottingham
NG8 1BB
E-mail: Angela.Smallwood@nottingham.ac.uk

Brenda Smith is Head of the Generic Centre of the Learning and Teaching
Support Network
Address: The Network Centre, Innovation Close, York Science Park,
Heslington, York YO10 5ZF
E-mail: brenda.smith@ltsn.ac.uk

Tan Oon Seng is Associate Professor of Psychological Studies at the
National Institute of Education at Nanyang Technological University,
Singapore
Address: 1 Nanyang Walk, Singapore 637616
E-mail: ostan@nie.edu.sg

Judith Thomas is Coordinator of the Regional Practice Teaching Centre in
the Faculty of Health and Social Care at the University of the West of
England
Address: Glenside Campus, Blackberry Hill, Bristol BS16 1DD
E-mail: judith.thomas@uwe.ac.uk

Tracey Varnava is Centre Manager and Research Coordinator for the UK
Centre for Legal Education
Address: University of Warwick, Coventry CV4 7AL
E-mail: t.varnava@warwick.ac.uk

James Wisdom is a Higher Education Consultant
Address: 25 Hartington Road, London W4 3TL
E-mail: jameswisdom@compuserve.com

Mantz Yorke is Director of the Centre for Higher Education Development
at Liverpool John Moores University
Address: I M Marsh Campus, Barkhill Road, Liverpool L17 6BD
E-mail: m.yorke@livjm.ac.uk

Preface

Carole Baume

This book is strongly based on the experience of practitioners. It comes out of the experiences of many people in the world of higher education who have tried to improve practice through educational development projects. The practices they have been addressing vary, as do the improvements they sought. The common thread is that they were involved in collaborative projects to find ways to make those improvements.

This book is not based on an extensive research programme. We looked for a literature based on research into project management in educational development projects, and failed to find very much that addressed our concerns and the concerns of project teams with which we worked. So we set about commissioning descriptions of project management. We present here the original descriptions together with our reflections on them.

This book does not need to be read from cover to cover. In the Introduction, Carole Baume introduces project management, first in general and then in the context of educational development projects. In Chapter 1, Paul Martin provides a brief history of national educational development initiatives in the UK. In each of Chapters 2 to 9, project managers tell their stories of the management of a project within the Higher Education Funding Council for England's (HEFCE's) Fund for the Development of Teaching and Learning (FDTL). Each chapter focuses on a particular aspect of project management. At the end of each of these chapters, the editors add a contextualizing commentary. The chapters focus as follows:

- Chapter 2: project planning;

- Chapter 3: the contribution of networking to project effectiveness;

- Chapter 4: the use of a project steering group;

- Chapter 5: the organization and financial skills required to run a project;

- Chapter 6: dealing with the inevitable changes in the life of a project;

- Chapter 7: effective working within the project team and the host institution;

- Chapter 8: approaches to dissemination of project outcomes; and

- Chapter 9: evaluation.

In Chapters 10 to 12, three authors give varied international perspectives on the management of projects. Finally, in Chapter 13, Mantz Yorke provides a conceptual overview to managing educational development projects and draws on the preceding chapters in offering some personal reflections.

How you approach this book will depend on your own particular interests:

- If you are the manager of a nationally funded project, you might be interested in the topics we have selected for special attention in Chapters 2 to 9 as well as in Chapter 12, which draws lessons for project management from varied projects in many countries.

- If you are a member of a project team, you might have a particular responsibility within the project and might select one or two of the chapters from 2 to 9, according to your responsibilities.

- If you are an institutional manager responsible for managing educational development projects within your institution, you should probably read the Introduction, Chapters 1 and 13, and dip into the remaining chapters to find suggestions on particular topics of concern to you.

- If you are the officer responsible for running an educational development national initiative, you will probably want to read the whole book and recommend it to the managers of projects within your initiative!

Acknowledgements

Many people have helped us, directly and indirectly, in the preparation of this book and it is only proper that we acknowledge their help. Our thanks, then, go to the following:

- To the authors of the various chapters, for being willing to put into the public domain their experiences with educational development projects, in order that others might benefit.

- To colleagues from the National Coordination Team for their general support, and for contributing to the commentaries at the end of the FDTL-based chapters. (Here, particular thanks to Alison Holmes and Rachel Segal.)

- To Gerry Taggart of HEFCE, for his long-standing commitment to maximizing the impact of FDTL.

- To Sarah Turpin, for her contribution to the shaping of the book by drawing on her experiences with the Teaching and Learning Technology programme.

- To James Wisdom, for his active contribution as Series Editor (which included hosting an early, formative – and highly enjoyable – meeting at his house on the bank of the Thames and also preparing the first draft of the index).

- To Carey Senter Associates, for their careful copy-editing of the text into its final form.

Introduction and overview

Carole Baume with Paul Martin

PROJECT MANAGEMENT

In the commercial world it has for many years been recognized that good project management is a key, if not the key, element in the success of projects. This is equally true in a public service environment like higher education (HE). But what do we mean by project management? And what is a project?

Change initiatives can take many forms, but projects are bounded by the constraints of objectives, timescale, context and budget. Viv Martin (2002) lists the attributes of a project as follows. A project:

- has a clear purpose that can be achieved in a limited time;
- has a clear end when the outcome has been achieved;
- is resourced to achieve specific outcomes;
- has someone acting as a sponsor or commissioner who expects the outcomes to be delivered on time;
- is a one-off activity and would not normally be repeated.

Though this definition of a project is non-specific, it accurately describes the nature of an educational development project of the type supported by the Fund for the Development of Teaching and Learning (FDTL). These projects have agreed objectives that are to be delivered within an agreed timescale, and they are resourced to achieve these objectives by a commissioner, in this case, the Higher Educational Funding Council for England (HEFCE). It is therefore reasonable to assume that if projects in educational development initiatives meet the above definition, then they will benefit from project management processes used in other sectors.

Elements of project management

There are a variety of project management models, but they generally include the following elements:

- defining objectives and outcomes;
- producing a project delivery plan;
- team building, leading and motivating;
- communication;
- monitoring and control;
- review and evaluation;
- exit strategy.

Let's consider each of these elements of general project management in a little more detail.

Defining the project objectives and outcomes clearly is vitally important as it enables the project leader and team to understand what they have to achieve, to plan how to achieve it and to know when they have got there. If the objectives and outcomes are not clear or achievable, then the project team will have problems interpreting and delivering the project and may fail to deliver in terms of the commissioner's expectations.

Producing a practical project delivery plan to the agreed timescale is the next essential step. Ideally this would involve the project team and any partner institutions. It is helpful if these same people can be part of the original team that defines the project outcomes. However, this is often not the case, and many project teams are brought together to take on an existing project. It is important that the project plan is a practical working document that enables the team to see where and when the main activities take place, and that within reason the project plan is flexible enough to change and develop as the project and its needs unfold. The plan can also form the basis of agreements or contracts for members of the team to deliver work to mutually agreed timescales.

Team building, leading and motivating are crucial parts of the project manager's role. Projects can have teams ranging from a few members to dozens, and it is important for the success of the project that everyone feels valued as a member of the team. This is best done if team members are involved in the project from the start and share the development role. As well as taking responsibility for the project, one of the main roles of project managers is leadership, helping to forge the vision, motivating the team and enabling them to deliver the outcomes. They need to supply the energy and support when the team is flagging, and to maintain the focus on the project outcomes.

Good communications are essential to a project team. If teams have a large number of members or are geographically scattered it becomes easy for individuals to feel left out. If regular communications are not maintained through team meetings, videoconferencing, phone calls or e-mails, work deadlines may slip or subgroups might go off-message. Good communications are also necessary with the project sponsors or commissioners, especially as most projects may require re-defining and re-negotiation in the light of interim project findings or changing circumstances. Communications should also extend to end-users if these are different from the sponsors. In general it is a good idea to develop good communications with any person or group who may be affected by the project, including stakeholders, partner institutions, and non-project colleagues who may be exasperated at your monopolizing the departmental fax machine!

For **monitoring and control** to be effective it is important that the project has clear and measurable objectives and outcomes and a detailed project plan. If these are in place it is possible for the project manager to monitor progress and expenditure against agreed objectives and time-scales, and to take any necessary action accordingly. With good communications and frequent team meetings, progress can be constantly monitored and reviewed in formal and informal ways, thus diminishing the likelihood of nasty surprises, and allowing early corrective action to be taken as problems arise.

Reviewing and evaluation are linked with the monitoring function. They are often seen as something that takes place at the end of the project to determine how well it has achieved its aims and objectives. However, by this time it may be too late! Review and evaluation should form part of an ongoing cycle throughout the life of the project, and should be used to adjust and improve the quality of the project's outcomes, increasing the chances of successful completion.

The exit strategy is important for two reasons. First, if the project is to effectively hand over or embed its learning within an organization, the team needs to plan this as part of the project process, not as a bolt-on when the project has finished. Second, the exit strategy is needed to make sure that the project does actually finish and finally reports, and that materials and other products are handed over to the necessary bodies.

It is evident from the model of project management discussed above that the project manager needs to have a considerable range of skills in order to bring a project to a successful conclusion. In the commercial world there is an understanding of the need for project management skills when tackling a large project. In education, however, project management was until recently mostly undertaken by academic staff skilled in teaching or research but without the experience or range of skills necessary to bring a project to a successful completion.

PROJECT MANAGEMENT AND EDUCATIONAL DEVELOPMENT

Later in this chapter you can read summaries of eight projects undertaken within the first phase of the FDTL, whose establishment is described in Chapter 1. In Chapters 2 to 9 you can read about these projects in more detail. Why did we choose these eight FDTL Phase One projects for this book from the existing 44? As these eight projects finished, their project managers and others were invited to a meeting to explore with members of the National Co-ordination Team (NCT) which aspects of project management had made a particular difference to them. They identified 13 aspects of project management which they believed were significant in the running of a successful project. These were:

- networking with other projects, other institutions, professional bodies and/ or national agencies using relevant networks and experts;

- recruiting and maintaining good support staff who are dedicated, effective, efficient and not set in their ways;

- good use of a well-constituted steering group ('well-constituted' includes 'high-level' members with a sufficient degree of externality to the project; 'good use' includes good documentation for meetings);

- organizational skills and planning (including clear planning, setting and keeping to targets and deadlines, good monitoring and reporting frameworks, and appropriate flexibility);

- financial skills (including having a strong grip and creatively using/ re-profiling project finances);

- being flexible to changes in circumstances (including being responsive to NCT suggestions, making creative responses to changing circumstances and exploiting new possibilities, being opportunistic, being good at seeing further potential in the project, and making good use of the results of formative evaluations);

- good relations between project manager and project director, and indeed among all project staff;

- good relations with the host institution (including getting further funding, getting and using support from the institution, using high-level support, and establishing good relationships with senior managers and with finance staff);

- clear roles and job specifications for all project members;

- exploring possible synergies within the project and with other projects and institutional strategies and priorities;

- clarity from the outset about project outcomes and methods;

- strong and imaginative dissemination of outcomes from an early stage;

- good use of evaluation, based on a clear account of project goals.

In talking through these issues of project management, the project managers and NCT members realized that eight FDTL projects together embodied and exemplified these 13 principles. In Chapters 2 to 9 you will encounter these aspects of project management through the stories of these eight FDTL projects. Given a very limited allocation of words, the authors were asked not to try to describe everything in their projects, but rather to focus on a particular aspect or aspects of project management, as shown in Table 0.1.

Each of these projects is unique. Each had its main base in a different institution. Each had a different educational purpose. Each was concerned to improve and disseminate further a different educational practice that had, through Teaching Quality Assessment, been judged as excellent.

However, the projects also have much in common. They were funded on the basis of a written application that had a clear template and explicit criteria for selection. The criteria included several aspects of project management. The projects were funded by the HEFCE for either two or three years. Most projects bid for, and were awarded, £250k in total.

The projects were supported by the National Co-ordination Team, based in the Centre for Higher Education Practice at the Open University. This team was appointed in February 1997, about six months after most of the projects had begun work. The work of the National Co-ordination Team in support of projects is discussed later in this chapter. Further information can be obtained from www.ncteam.ac.uk.

Table 0.1   *The chapters and their project management issues*

Chapter	Project	Institution	Project management topics
2	Sharing Excellence	Nottingham Trent University	Recruiting and maintaining **good support staff** who are dedicated, effective, efficient and not set in their ways. **Good relations with the host institution**. **Clear roles and job specifications** for all project members. **Clarity** from the outset about project outcomes and methods.
3	Effective Project Work in Computer Science (EPCOS)	University of Kent at Canterbury	**Networking** with other projects, other institutions, professional bodies and/or national agencies using relevant networks and experts. **Exploring possible synergies** within the project and with other projects and institutional strategies and priorities.
4	Personal and Academic Development for Students in Higher Education (PADSHE)	University of Nottingham	Good use of a well-constituted **steering group**.
5	National Centre for Legal Education (NCLE)	University of Warwick	**Organizational skills and planning**. **Financial skills**.
6	Teaching and Learning at the Environment–Science–Society Interface (TALESSI)	University of Greenwich	**Being flexible to changes in circumstances**.
7	Self Assessment in Professional and Higher Education (SAPHE)	University of Bristol	**Good relations with the host institution**. Recruiting and maintaining **good support staff** who are dedicated, effective, efficient and not set in their ways.
8	Dissemination of Good Teaching, Learning and Assessment Practices in Geography	Cheltenham and Gloucester College of Higher Education (now University of Gloucestershire)	Strong and imaginative **dissemination** of outcomes from an early stage.
9	History 2000: developing reflective practice throughout the discipline	Bath Spa College	**Clarity** from the outset about project outcomes and methods. Good use of **evaluation**, based on a clear account of project goals.

'Sharing Excellence' at Nottingham Trent University, described in Chapter 2

This two-year project was based on the teaching enhancement that had been shown through the use of peer observation. Unusually, this project was based wholly within a single institution (Nottingham Trent University) – most FDTL projects operate across two or more institutions. As the project developed, the focus broadened out to encompass a range of particular teaching and learning issues that had surfaced during discussions following peer observations. These issues included student assessment and gaining feedback from students. Brenda Smith's chapter details the importance of laying the ground well for such a project.

'Effective Project Work in Computer Science' (EPCOS) at the University of Kent at Canterbury, described in Chapter 3

This project built on the work of an existing network of teachers of Computer Science. When asked what would make the biggest difference to the experience of their students, they chose student project work as the focus for this three-year project. The consortium involved in this project involved departments across England. Sally Fincher's chapter focuses on the importance of networking for this project, and the methods employed to sustain it.

'Personal and Academic Development for Students in Higher Education' (PADSHE) at the University of Nottingham, described in Chapter 4

Records of achievement and personal profiling were the starting points for this project from an English department. Working with four other universities, this project team developed computer- and paper-based systems for what have come to be called 'progress files', and helped other universities to develop locally appropriate versions. Angela Smallwood's chapter explores the value to this process of a well-constituted steering group.

'National Centre for Legal Education' (NCLE) at University of Warwick, described in Chapter 5

This project was set up to allow a greater focus on the practice of legal education in higher education and developed a range of materials on particular topics of teaching and learning in Law. It developed into the Learning and Teaching Support Network (LTSN) subject centre for Law.

Tracey Varnava's chapter focuses on the important, but often over-looked, organizational and financial skills involved in managing a project.

'Teaching and Learning at the Environment–Science–Society Interface' (TALESSI) at the University of Greenwich, described in Chapter 6

This ambitious project explored the topic of interdisciplinarity in higher education. Working with a growing group of enthusiasts in other universities, the project team developed and tested a range of teaching and learning resources to encourage teachers to take a more interdisciplinary approach to their subjects. June Balshaw and Howard Senter's chapter considers some of the flexibility needed in a project when, as is almost inevitable, the unfolding of the project leads to divergences from the original project plan.

'Self Assessment in Professional and Higher Education' (SAPHE) at the University of Bristol, described in Chapter 7

Working with three departments of Social Work and three departments of Law, this three-year project took the issue of self-assessment as its focus. Materials for use by teachers and students, scholarly articles, workshops and conferences were used to explore and extend the use of self-assessment. Judith Thomas's chapter looks at the impact of working effectively with people within the project team and in the institutions as a whole.

'Dissemination of Good Teaching, Learning and Assessment Practices in Geography' run by the Geography Discipline Network (GDN), based at Cheltenham and Gloucester College of Higher Education (now University of Gloucestershire), described in Chapter 8

The Geography Discipline Network grew from an earlier nationally funded project. It brought together leading geography educators with educational developers to produce a set of guides on teaching and learning topics such as fieldwork and assessment. It subsequently developed into part of the Geography, Environmental and Earth Sciences LTSN subject centre. Phil Gravestock's chapter is concerned with making an impact through dissemination. He uses a model first developed by Sally Fincher of the University of Kent to stress the importance of disseminating the work of such a project.

'History 2000: developing reflective practice throughout the discipline', based at Bath Spa College, described in Chapter 9

History 2000 approached the issue of improving the quality of teaching in History by setting up several mini-projects in history departments throughout England. James Wisdom's chapter is informed therefore by the experience of evaluating the project as a whole, as well as many different approaches taken to the evaluation of the sub-projects within History 2000.

SUPPORTING PROJECT MANAGEMENT THROUGH COORDINATION

The version of project management outlined above works in a particular context, that of a number of projects being undertaken within a common framework, with central support and coordination. The National Co-ordination Team was set up in February 1997 with five main intentions:

- to maximize the quality of elements of the FDTL programme as a whole;

- to maximize value for money from FDTL;

- to help FDTL to operate as effectively as possible;

- to ensure that the outcomes of the programme are more than the sum of the individual projects;

- to ensure the maximum impact on learning and teaching across higher education.

In a little more detail:

- The quality of elements of the programme would be maximized by employing an information, communications and support strategy. This would ensure the wide availability of accurate and up-to-date information, rapid and focused communications within and among the many constituencies involved, and proven high quality educational development support for individual projects and institutions.

- Value for money was to be maximized by working at two levels. One was to help individual projects to develop and implement rigorous and appropriate management systems, to specify outcomes and plans, to manage their resources, keep to schedule and keep within budget, and to make appropriate changes to plans, maintain records and report progress. The second level was to apply these same processes to the activities of the NCT, for example by continually streamlining systems and by targeting projects most in need of support.

- To help FDTL to operate as effectively as possible, the NCT would support the HEFCE and the Department for Education Northern Ireland, reporting to the HEFCE management committee on the progress of projects and programmes and, where appropriate, making suggestions for change or for new initiatives.

- To ensure that the whole would be more than the sum of the parts, the NCT planned to help projects to develop fruitful working relations with each other, and to use and support their professional and subject bodies and regional and national development agencies.

- Maximum impact on learning and teaching across higher education was to be achieved by promoting the work of the FDTL programme using a wide range of targeted media to reach the many different audiences in the sector. At the level of individual projects, each project would be helped to focus on disseminating its outcomes in ways that would maximize the likelihood of their being used (rather than being glanced at and then discarded).

Many educational development projects are undertaken without the benefit of such an overall support and coordination function. However, some of the coordination functions described above can be achieved on a smaller scale with less sophisticated mechanisms. Two examples are as follows:

First, where more than one educational development project is being undertaken in an institution (and this is hopefully always the case!), then the projects should be strongly encouraged to liaise with each other and to share good practice in at least some of the areas considered in this chapter.

Second, where an educational development project involves a particular or professional area, then those working on the project should be encouraged to identify projects in the same discipline or professional area in other institutions or national professional bodies, and to work with them.

Further, any project is likely to benefit from professional help with dissemination, which might be provided through an educational development unit, perhaps with the support of a publicity department within an institution.

REFERENCE

Martin V (2002) *Managing Projects in Health and Social Care*, Routledge, London

1

The rise of national educational development projects

Paul Martin

INTRODUCTION

The story of National Educational Development project initiatives within higher education in the UK has been one of often-bold innovation in response to powerful socio-economic imperatives caused by the twin pressures of the globalization of capitalism and the rapid speed of technological change. This chapter explores this socio-economic and political context, and it then goes on to describe the major initiatives, commenting on their strengths and weaknesses and charting the emergence of good project management as a recognized key element in the success of such projects.

SOCIO-ECONOMIC AND POLITICAL CONTEXT OF THE RISE OF NATIONAL EDUCATIONAL DEVELOPMENT PROJECTS WITHIN THE UK

During the immediate post Second World War period, Canada, Australia and the UK rapidly expanded university and teacher training college provision, initially to meet the needs of returning ex-servicemen and women. Higher education (HE) student numbers in the UK grew from 85,000 in 1950 to 443,000 in 1970 (Miller, 1995a: 42). The main drivers for this huge and continuing expansion of numbers arose from a series of global social, economic and technological pressures that impacted on UK society. A period of relative economic prosperity in the UK enabled the development and implementation of an idealistic social agenda that attempted to create what Miller (1995b) termed a more meritocratic and fairer society. This resulted in a major force for change in opening up access to HE to more people. Alongside this, governments were increasingly seeing education as a way of supporting economic development, and the Robins Report in 1963 'legitimized a pattern of expansion founded on the double grounds of student demand and the needs of the economy' (quoted in Miller, 1995b: 14). The expansion in student numbers was enabled by the expansion of existing universities, the building of new universities and, from 1964 onwards, the establishment of 29 polytechnics by the Labour government under Harold Wilson. The Open University was also founded in this round of expansion to provide part-time distance learning for those who could not abandon family and career to attend university full-time.

By the middle of the following decade the energy crisis of the 1970s and the subsequent world economic downturn had damaged the UK economy so much that the Labour government began cuts in education and social services. Purvis and Walford observed that during this time the economic problems and 'a growing disenchantment with education ... brought with them renewed attempts by pressure groups and policy makers to strengthen the links between education and the economy' (Purvis and Walford, quoted in Pollard, 1988: 4). In 1976 the Prime Minister James Callaghan delivered his now famous 'Ruskin Speech' in which he blamed the education system for failing to provide British industry with the skilled workforce it required. By implication this skills deficit was the cause of British industry's failure to compete successfully in world markets and thus a contributing factor in the rise of unemployment and ensuing social problems. The clear message to education was that it should be turning out people with the skills needed by industry for the country's economic and social health.

As Jarvis argues, 'the policies of the United Kingdom government in the 1980s and early 1990s have been designed to redirect education away from individual needs, to the demands of the industrial and commercial sector of society' (Jarvis, 1993: 48). The new Conservative government under Margaret Thatcher in 1979 brought into play the monetarist philosophy of Milton Friedman. It continued the cuts in government funding, partly through economic necessity, but also in an attempt to make HE less dependent on central funds and to force greater links and support from industry. It also began the drive for greater accountability in the use of public funds and, later, continued pressure for greater student access to and participation in HE, but with a firm vocational direction (implicitly acknowledging human capital theory). By the late 1980s there was a renewed recognition of the desirability of increasing participation in HE, which was alluded to in the government White Paper *Higher Education: Meeting the challenge* (DES, 1987). The White Paper and subsequent 1992

Education Act stressed what Miller calls 'the need for increased efficiency in Higher Education, if the expansion was to be achieved without loss of quality' (Miller, 1995b: 17). The Act also put in place new arrangements for 'quality assurance and audit of teaching and research'.

Alongside the rise of socio-economic pressures on HE came the equally powerful effects from the increasing speed of change in the field of science and technology. Toffler realized, as early as 1970, that 'the rapid obsolescence of knowledge and the extension of the life span make it clear that the skills learned in youth are unlikely to remain relevant by the time old age arrives' (Toffler, 1970: 368). Here he raises issues about the changing nature of knowledge which, in many fields, has a decreasing life span. And the educationalist Malcolm Knowles points to the educational problems this creates, which relate to the practicality and cost of ongoing updating. Knowles observes that if we are to 'avoid the catastrophe of human obsolescence' (Knowles, 1990), then the prevailing deficit model of education needs to be changed to one of lifelong learning. Knowles had argued previously that:

> It is no longer functional to define education as a process of transmitting what is known; it must now be defined as a lifelong process of enquiry. And so the most important learning of all – for both children and adults – is learning how to learn, the skills of self-directed enquiry.
>
> (Knowles, 1980: 41)

As the speed and nature of both knowledge and the social world change increasingly quickly and become more complex, members of society need to be able to learn for themselves and become self-directed in their enquiry. In addition, a larger proportion of the population than in previous times needs to attain a higher level of education to function in society and to help keep it economically viable in the global marketplace.

Governments have attempted to address these problems by a range of strategies. First, teachers at all levels of education have been encouraged to develop in their students a series of transferable skills and self-direction in learning, in an attempt to develop a population that can engage in lifelong learning both inside and outside the formal education system. Second, what Barnett (1994) calls the 'elite to mass change' has been promoted in order to engage a greater percentage of the population in both further and higher education. This has been done in an attempt to avoid the danger of socio-economic 'obsolescence' in society of many of its members, and increase the country's economic competitiveness within the global economy. Both of these strategies are reflected in the various national educational development initiatives that have been at the forefront of introducing new practice into the HE sector.

Initially the 'elite to mass' movement was driven by ideals of creating a fairer society, though it was always accompanied by concepts of increasing human capital for the economy. The idealistic rationale was, however, gradually overshadowed by the socio-economic imperative, and was joined from the late 1970s by a growing agenda of efficiency. Though these latter drivers were originally created as a response to economic crisis, cost effectiveness became part of government ideology drawn from a monetarist philosophy, and it became embedded in the managerial approach to government from the late 1980s. The effect on HE of the combination of the expansion of student numbers with calls for increased efficiency has been a dramatic increase in teaching loads and class sizes, which in turn has led to initiatives to help develop teaching and learning strategies that can help teachers to cope while maintaining standards. The scale of the increase in student numbers is shown by the figures: at the time of Robbins, one in 16 of people in the 18-to-30 age range was a student, compared with one in three now. This increase in student numbers has also meant that whereas 50 years ago HE dealt with a narrow band of students selected from the very ablest, the broadening of participation has led to the admission of students with a wider range of abilities. This, in turn, has created a need to develop a range of new practices and systems to support students in their studies.

NATIONAL EDUCATIONAL DEVELOPMENT PROJECTS AND THE RISE OF EDUCATIONAL PROJECT MANAGEMENT

Since the late 1980s there has been a series of government-led National Educational Development initiatives which were intended to help address the issues raised by the 'elite to mass' agenda and the economic imperative. The focuses of these initiatives have been to make education more relevant to economic needs, and to expand numbers of participants in HE through increased efficiency, without losing quality and within a budget that the country can afford. Various initiatives have attempted to research into, to develop and to disseminate ways in which new technologies and best practice in teaching and learning can assist in these aims.

In the late 1980s the Manpower Services Commission attempted to introduce the new agenda into further education (FE) and HE via National Vocational Qualifications (NVQs), and although this had considerable success in the FE sector, it made little impact in HE. The Training Agency's **Enterprise in Higher Education** (EHE) initiative was launched in December 1987 by the Secretary of State for Employment, though it soon became embedded in the Department of Education. It was the first government initiative aimed specifically at tackling issues related to expanding HE and making it more relevant to economic needs. Harvey and Knight (1996) observed that although the original aim of EHE was to encourage qualities of enterprise in students in HE, there had been a 'focus on the development of personal skills related to future employment, curriculum change and staff development all of which suggests that EHE has a wider role as an agent of institutional change' (Harvey and Knight, 1996: 76–77).

In an attempt to bring about these changes in the teaching/learning relationship and to orient HE more towards industry and enterprise, the government invested £50 million in the EHE initiative, offering up to £1 million per institution for specific projects. A total of 59 projects were funded over the life of the initiative. Although commentators disagree as to the overall effectiveness and impact of the EHE initiative, Wright observed that EHE 'exerted significant pressure for change in curricula and forms of learning within UK higher education' (Wright, 1992: 218), but the overall effects were 'constrained' by structural factors within the HE system. Perhaps its most important contribution, as Wright suggests, is that it encouraged a 'dialogue between academics and employers and, by concentrating on the question of to what extent, and how, higher education should serve the world of employment, has begun to encourage the HE system to develop a new, self-conscious and publicly-accessible vision of its own mission' (Wright, 1992: 219).

The contemporary but smaller **Higher Education for Capability Initiative** was launched in 1989 by the Royal Society of Arts (RSA) 10 years after the publication of its manifesto in 1979. The manifesto, signed by 250 well-known figures from industry, commerce and public life, focused attention on what they saw as a disproportionate emphasis that the education system placed on 'comprehension and cultivation' and the pursuit of a 'scholarly path'. They felt that a greater emphasis should be placed on preparation for life in the outside world, which is a reflection of the increasing demands for education to support the needs of the national economy. However, Barnett observed a crucial philosophical difference between the Capability and Enterprise initiatives, saying that 'whereas Enterprise looked to create a particular set of skills, capacities and attitudes (of an enterprising character), Capability seeks to invade wider spheres of the mind' (Barnett, 1994: 94).

Though Capability was far less well endowed financially than EHE it managed to support a variety of activities over the three years of its existence, and collected over 400 examples of developments of capability in practice. Although as Barnett observes, it is difficult to disentangle the impact of 'Capability' from that of the 'Enterprise' initiative, in Weil's assessment the 'RSA Capability initiative has perhaps done little more than to stimulate and give substance to an argument about how learning and quality might be enhanced' (Weil, 1992: 200). However, the Capability ethos is still alive in some HE institutions that continue to carry the banner, and the issues it raised are very much alive within the areas of 'key skills' and employability, which form the focus of many projects in the Fund for the Development of Teaching and Learning (FDTL) Phase Three and figure strongly in FDTL Phase Four.

Recognition of the contribution of project management

By the time the **Teaching and Learning Technology Programme** (TLTP) was launched in 1992 by the Universities Funding Council (UFC), a combination of factors led to the setting up of a small team whose brief was to monitor and support the project's development. The factors were: the influence of managerialism and value for money within government; and the beginnings of recognition that large educational development initiatives needed some form of organization and support. The establishment of this team heralded a recognition within the funding body that project management was an important factor in the success of projects.

The main aim of TLTP was 'making teaching and learning more productive and efficient by harnessing modern technology'. The first two phases of the programme received £70 million and involved 76 projects which engaged in developing new technology-based materials for teaching and learning, and in exploring different approaches to the implementation of these materials on an institution-wide basis. Of these projects, 64 worked in consortia ranging from 3 to 50 institutional members, with grants ranging from £35,000 to £1,000,000. Phase Three of TLTP was begun in 1998 with the Higher Education Funding Council for England (HEFCE) and the Department for Education for Northern Ireland (DENI) funding a total of 32 projects with up to £3.5 million committed annually over three years. The emphasis was moved from the development of materials to the implementation and embedding of technology-based materials in higher education teaching and learning, and the evaluation of its effectiveness.

The **Effective Teaching and Assessment Programme** (ETAP) was created by the UFC in part to counter charges that it had spent too much on the TLTP and not enough on other aspects of Teaching and Learning. It was pointed out that the only thing being funded by the UFC was technology, whereas the main problem, created by a combination of increasing HE student numbers and drives for greater efficiency in teaching, was how to teach larger classes effectively. Most of the solutions to this problem are not technological – expensive in terms of hardware, software and training – but lie in teaching and learning practice. ETAP was set up with £1,000,000 for one year compared to TLTP with nearly £80 million invested in it, and ran a total of five projects. It had no formal coordination or support such as had been developed for TLTP and the later FTDL programmes, and there was little evaluation or dissemination of its outcomes.

The UFC funded several major development initiatives at this time including TLTP and Computers in Teaching Initiative (CTI) but none of this money went to polytechnics. When the binary system of funding was abandoned and the UFC and Polytechnics and Colleges Funding Council (PCFC) were joined under the new Higher Education Funding Council, the money for these initiatives stayed with the universities. The PCFC only funded one project at a cost of £100,000. This was called 'Teaching More Students', and was based at Oxford Brookes University. The project succeeded in putting 9,500 HE staff nationwide through workshops to help them to improve their teaching of large student groups.

Although the aims of EHE, Capability for HE and ETAP were laudable enough, their combined effect was limited. This was partly because of the resistance of HE to change, and partly because the idea of project management within the HE sector was not fully understood or recognized as a necessary factor for success. Money was awarded for good ideas through unfocused bidding processes and with little monitoring other than financial probity. With little or no history of project management within the HE sector, academics who led early projects often had little or no experience of project management processes and little experience to call on within their institutions. Also, although the initiatives had monitoring in the form of audit, they did not provide any active support to projects in relation to the process of running projects. The TLTP initiative was the first to have a small team attached to it, not only to monitor its progress but to support the project process.

In 1995 HEFCE and DENI launched the **Fund for the Development of Teaching and Learning** (FDTL). FDTL grew out of the key premise that rather than develop new practice in teaching and learning, the identification of existing good practice through the process of Teaching Quality Assessment (TQA) could lead to its dissemination to other institutions in the HE sector. It was envisaged as a system that could spread identified good practice from institutions with a high TQA score in this field to those that had achieved less well, with an accent on dissemination rather than development.

The main aims were to:

- stimulate developments in learning and teaching;
- secure the widest possible involvement of institutions in the take up and implementation of best practice;
- establish a clear link between quality assessment results and funding for teaching.

All rounds of FDTL have required institutions to have been recognized as 'excellent' under the original quality assessment regime, or to have gained a Teaching Quality Assessment grade of 4 in the aspect of provision for which funding was being sought, reflecting the intention to transfer good practice. However, as the initiative has developed, it has become evident that the notion of the transfer of good practice from one institution with a high score to another with a lower score was too simplistic, as contexts and circumstances between institutions and subjects are so varied. HEFCE has responded by broadening the criteria for inclusion in project partnerships to include institutions with lower grades, FE institutions with HE, and even industry and professional bodies, in recognition of the complexity of the issues and changing needs of the sector.

In Phase One of FDTL, 44 projects were funded at a cost of £8.5 million, and in Phase Two, 19 projects were funded costing a total of £4 million and covering specifically targeted subject areas. Currently, 33 projects are running as part of Phase Three, with Phase Four starting in the autumn of 2002 with funding of £8 million.

Lessons from previous initiatives had clearly been learnt by the funding bodies, and six months after the FDTL initiative was launched, HEFCE advertised for a National Co-ordinator to support the development of the projects and monitor their progress. This led to the setting up of the National Co-ordination Team (NCT) in February 1997. The TLTP support team joined the NCT to create a larger team which oversaw both initiatives, and which has developed a broad programme of project management workshops, briefing documents, a news bulletin and a Web site to support the project teams in their work.

An evaluation of FDTL Phases One and Two published by HEFCE and DENI in November 1998 reported that:

> In general FDTL projects – although often under pressure – do not demonstrate such naivety [as TLTP], partly because of the strong and effective support of NCT [National Co-ordination Team], and partly because most projects involve staff interested in the process of teaching and learning rather than the application of technology. Moreover the Council and NCT appear to have learned a number of lessons from previous initiatives which have ensured a higher level of central guidance and co-ordination of projects.
>
> (HEFCE, 1998: iii–iv)

Though not specifically mentioned in this report, the improvements were underpinned by the development of project management skills, experience within the project teams and professional support in the form of the NCT.

At the beginning of 2001 the latest round of projects to be funded under the Higher Education Innovations Fund were transferred from the Department for Education and Employment (DfEE) to HEFCE. These projects, involving FE and HE as well as industry, are related to issues of employability with the aim of developing key skills, employment skills and personal transferable skills within the student body. To support the development of the projects an Innovations Team (IT) was formed from elements from within the three existing experienced HEFCE coordination teams: the Teaching Quality Enhancement Fund (TQEF) National Co-ordination Team (NCT), the National Disability Team (NDT) and the Action on Access Team (AoA).

The transfer not only enabled the projects to work together with other similar initiatives such as FDTL and TLTP but also allowed the coordination teams to work together and share both their specific expertise and their different approaches to project management.

CONCLUSION

It is clear from this short and selective history of national education development initiatives that the issue of project management has grown over the past 20 years to become recognized as a key element in the success of projects. Alongside this, funding bodies have also developed an awareness that external support for projects in the form of the coordination teams is also a contributing factor in success.

In an evaluation report for HEFCE of FDTL projects it was stated that 'the need for effective project management is a consistent finding from many council evaluations' (HEFCE, 1998). The emergence of national educational project management support teams such as the National Co-ordination Team, the National Disability Team, and the Action on Access team has been in recognition of and direct response to this observed need. If funded projects are to achieve their full potential, then they need good project management to make them effective and to help maximize their impact.

REFERENCES

Barnett, R (1994) *The Limits of Competence*, Society for Research into Higher Education (SRHE) and Open University Press, Buckingham

Department of Education and Science (DES) (1987) White Paper, *Higher Education: Meeting the challenge*, DES, London

Harvey, L and Knight, P (1996) *Transforming Higher Education*, SRHE and Open University Press, Buckingham

Higher Education Funding Council for England (HEFCE) (1998) *Evaluation of the Fund for the Development of Teaching and Learning* (98/68), HEFCE Publications, Bristol

Jarvis, P (1993) *Adult Education and the State*, Routledge, London

Knowles, M (1980) *The Modern Practice of Adult Education*, Cambridge UP, New York

Knowles, M (1990) Fostering competence in self-directed learning, in *Learning to Learn Across the Lifespan*, ed R M Smith, Jossey Bass, Oxford

Miller, H (1995a) States, Economies and the Changing Labour Process of Academics: Australia, Canada and the United Kingdom, in *Academic Work*, ed J Smyth, SRHE and the OU Press, Buckingham, pp 40–59

Miller H (1995b) *The Management of Change in Universities*, SRHE and Open University Press, Buckingham

Pollard, A (1988) *Education and Training: the new vocationalism*, Open University Press, Milton Keynes

Toffler, A (1970) *Future Shock*, 1980 edn, Pan Books, London

Weil, S (1992) Creating capability for change in Higher Education: the RSA initiative, in *Learning to Effect*, ed R Barnett, SRHE and Open University Press, Buckingham, pp 186–203

Wright, P (1992) Learning through enterprise: the Enterprise in Higher Education initiative, in *Learning to Effect*, ed R Barnett, SRHE and Open University Press, Buckingham, pp 204–223

2

Project planning, visioning and being clear at the outset

Brenda Smith

This chapter is designed to save you time. It is based on the Japanese car principle of 60:40 (the split between designing and manufacturing). That means 60 per cent of time planning the project enables you to spend 40 per cent delivering it – the key point being that time invested in planning pays dividends later on: the point is elaborated below. The chapter, which is based on experience with the Sharing Excellence project at Nottingham Trent University (NTU), also illustrates the need to be flexible and the importance of adapting the project in the light of experience and of local and national developments. But it carries a health warning. Project planning and delivery can be time consuming and stressful. However, a project successfully delivered can be one of the most exhilarating, rewarding and effective forms of team working and continuing professional development that you will experience.

Clear planning and development are essential if positive outcomes are to be achieved. The following five stages are proposed as a basis for the development of the project planning:

1   Form the 'Think Tank' team.

2   Understand and clarify the criteria.

3   Produce clear aims and objectives.

4   Draft and redraft the plan.

5   Understand and apply the management of change.

In this chapter, I intersperse the lessons I have learnt from the project with brief accounts of what actually happened.

STAGE ONE: FORM THE 'THINK TANK' TEAM

Once the invitation to bid has been received, it is important to gather together a small team that will contribute to the project proposal. This helps to create joint ownership early on, even though this team might not be the staff who actually deliver the project. You may have a very clear idea about what you personally want, but listening to and incorporating the views of other staff will strengthen the proposal and lead to more creative ideas.

As soon as the FDTL Phase One funding proposals became known, I invited a small group of staff representing the eligible subject areas to an initial meeting. Nottingham Trent University was eligible to bid for funding because external quality reviewers had rated the Nottingham Business School and the Department of Chemistry as excellent. Other departments that had been commended for aspects of good practice were also included. As external funding could only be obtained in respect of those departments that had been assessed, the university provided some additional funding so as to ensure that every faculty was represented by at least one of its departments, and to ensure a spread of coverage across the university. It also demonstrated commitment from senior managers which, I believe, was a key factor in managing change across an institution such as Nottingham Trent.

Those new to project management may have to work at developing good contacts with one or more senior managers. If this is not easy, then working with someone who has these contacts is important. Working with senior managers can lead to that group of staff having more effective ownership of, and involvement in, the project. If managers see themselves as playing a key role in the project, then your success is their success. However, this involvement needs nurturing and sustaining: it means keeping them involved at every stage of development, seeking their advice and giving them credit where appropriate. All of this is time consuming but nevertheless certainly worthwhile. The experience and advice of senior managers can greatly enhance project development and outcomes, and bring a different perspective to the project.

At this first meeting the institutional subject reports were analysed and possible themes identified via a brainstorming session. Eventually peer observation of teaching became the agreed theme, as good staff development practices had been identified in all the reports. The idea of peer observation was not new to Nottingham Trent University. Two pilot schemes had already been undertaken, in the Nottingham Business School and the Department of Computing. It therefore seemed opportune that, when funding became available, peer observation of teaching should be the theme that could embrace every faculty in the university.

STAGE TWO: UNDERSTAND AND CLARIFY THE CRITERIA

It is essential to clarify the specified bid criteria early in the planning process. It is all too easy to go off on a tangent thinking about lots of wonderful projects that staff would like to create. All Think Tank members need a shared understanding of what the criteria do, and do not, allow in order to give a focus to the discussions. Possible topic areas can then be considered. However, the group also needs to think strategically. What are the key issues for the institution or department, and how can your project become an integral part of that strategic planning process? For some members of the team, thinking strategically may be new, perhaps because they have previously concentrated on their specific course and have not been aware of key strategic issues at university level. It is important at this stage therefore that, to provide the strategic dimension, a senior manager is involved.

Newcomers to project planning are often amazed at how long this process can take. It is useful to schedule a set number of meetings into the diary. The importance of refreshments should not be underestimated. Staff who are willing to make a contribution need some consideration, especially if they are working late.

A useful technique we employed at this point was to list the criteria and then briefly explain each point, to ensure understanding. For example, differentiating between an aim and an objective will be new to some staff. Going through the criteria point by point also ensures that none of them is omitted. Encourage creative ideas at this stage, as they may prove very useful later on. For example, once we had decided on the topic of peer observation of teaching, one member of the team suggested we should appoint a coordinator (a recent graduate) to work with students. This proved an excellent suggestion and demonstrated the value of group members contributing to the project plan. It is also important to allow everyone to have his or her say, since this helps to engender shared ownership of the decision making. Resentment can build up if colleagues feel they are not being listened to.

By the end of this second stage (if not before) a clear theme should have emerged, which has been checked out against all the criteria. Appointing someone within the team to take on the specific responsibility of checking that the proposal fits the criteria helps to prevent the team going off at a tangent.

STAGE THREE: PRODUCE CLEAR AIMS AND OBJECTIVES

The third stage is to be specific about what you want to achieve. If the project is to be successful, what will it look like at the end? What will you take as your indicators of success? A clear aim and specific objectives are necessary to guide the direction of the project, even though these might be modified during the planning and delivery stages.

Think through each objective – how will you know if you have been successful? What indicators of success will you use? If these indicators of success do not come quickly to mind, it may be because the objectives lack specificity and need rethinking. Objectives then need developing into a clear plan. At this stage one person needs to take responsibility for producing the first draft.

Once the first draft is produced it is much easier for the team to discuss the proposals. The use of a flip chart during discussions helps the group to keep track of the unfolding of ideas. Again it is helpful if one person makes the modifications and circulates the copy around the group before the next meeting.

To develop the plan, a useful technique is to take each area that needs to be addressed in the application, and to concentrate on one section at a time. However, do not feel that when you are discussing the plan you have to stick rigidly to the order required for the bid (although we ended up with a final plan in the order requested and I would suggest that you do the same).

We asked ourselves what we wanted to produce at the end of the project, and how we would know if we had been successful. In other words, we looked at the deliverables and then worked backwards, looking at how we might achieve the outcomes. For example, consider the practicalities of peer observation. What materials are required? If peers are be encouraged to participate, staff need guidelines on what the process is about and what the benefits are for them. How is the process to be conducted: are there any ethical issues? What about observation sheets: how is the process to be recorded and will it be confidential? The answers to questions like these will all influence the thinking process and the outputs produced.

Whereas thinking about aims and objectives was relatively easy, addressing implementation issues was more complex. For example, how could the emerging Sharing Excellence project ensure that staff were adequately trained in the processes both of observing and of being observed? This involves some key skills, and in addition it takes time to build up participants' confidence. Training materials need to be produced. The idea was for the project team to prepare these materials once we had secured funding. The project manager would then train the trainers, who would in turn work with staff at the local level. There would be an opportunity to modify both the training and the delivery according to local needs. This methodology proved to be highly successful. Each faculty coordinator contributed his or her special talent, from which the team as a whole benefited. One coordinator put all the materials – including interesting and relevant articles – together in a training file. That led to a sharing of materials across faculties, and encouraged staff to read some pedagogical literature. Spending some funding on relevant books helped staff keep up to date with pedagogical developments in the relevant field and encouraged staff to read around different topic areas.

The giving and receiving of feedback was another issue. To help to develop observation skills we showed a number of externally produced videos to other NTU colleagues participating in the project. These videos demonstrated staff teaching in different subject areas and in different ways. We then posed to these colleagues a set of questions, such as:

- How would you ensure that the person on the video started by giving an analysis of how he or she felt the session had gone?

- What questions might you ask?

- What positive feedback would you give to this member of staff?

- What did the person feel had not gone so well, and what might be a possible solution?

- If the person was to repeat the session, what might he or she do differently?

- How might you ensure that the person being observed left with a clear indication of what went well, and one thing he or she might do differently or better as a result of this feedback?

Using videos of people our colleagues did not know helped to reduce the potential tension, and was more likely to have an impact on future observations. Practising giving feedback about someone on a video is certainly less threatening than doing so 'live'. This practice also helped staff to develop their confidence in giving feedback: it is not an easy process, but it is a skill that can be developed with practice.

A suggestion here is to tabulate these objectives against the primary indicators of success: this enables you to test your objectives against your outcomes.

We ended up with the following aims for the Sharing Excellence project:

- To share actively the skills and good practices that led to the designation of 'excellence' for learning and teaching both internally and externally.

- To encourage the creation of a university-wide culture that recognizes and rewards excellence in teaching and learning.

- To provide a network of support and exchanges of good practice by peer observation of teaching.

- To provide a more effective system of both staff and student feedback.

- To develop a teaching portfolio.

STAGE FOUR: DRAFT AND REDRAFT THE PLAN

By the fourth stage you may be wondering if you will ever actually produce the plan, but be prepared to draft and redraft it. It can be a long process and you need to build this time into your planning process. As I remarked earlier, time spent planning really pays dividends. Once you know your funding is secured, your targets and project plan give you a clear starting point and direction, and you can begin immediately.

Establishing a working title during the planning stage gives the project a sense of identity. A short, catchy title is also good for promotional purposes.

Local flexibility is really important. Different departments and subject areas may have different cultural norms and ways of working. These need to be respected and built upon. The proposal was for each subject area to select 20 staff who would form themselves into small groups of three or four. These small groups were then supported by the relevant faculty coordinator (the faculty coordinators along with the project manager, internal evaluator, student coordinator and administrator formed the project team). Within these small groups of four or five staff, each member would be observed twice by colleagues from other groups and would, in turn, observe members of two other groups. The teaching situation selected would be left to the discretion of the staff concerned. For example, English staff decided that they wanted to focus on small-group and seminar work for their observations. They felt they would benefit by having a more specific focus to their work. They wanted to see how staff could ensure student cooperation, group involvement, and how they could motivate all students to come well prepared. Other subject areas wanted to observe the large lecture, as this was the area in which they felt they had most to learn.

Sometimes a proposal can be too rigid, in that it expects all departments or institutions to follow the same path. A few diversions, and being flexible, can produce more effective results for all concerned. It is not a weakness or an indication of poor planning to modify activities along the way. Rather it is a sign of confidence to make alterations in the light of experience.

Another example of the importance of being flexible occurred when we were planning the observation sheets. The original idea was to produce a university observation sheet that all staff could use. After all, that would be a neat solution. However, after much discussion we could not agree. And we finally realized that it did not matter. We did not need to agree on a common format. If English staff wanted a blank sheet of paper and the engineers wanted a detailed checklist, then that was the way forward. It was a turning point for the group and a recognition of the need to be responsive to the local context. If staff feel secure with their chosen methodology, then they are more likely to take on ownership and make it work successfully. This flexibility could easily be applied when working with different universities.

Visualizing and thinking through the consequences of an action can be a useful technique for checking whether your plan will work. For example, how might the teaching observation described above work in practice? Does your project plan cause problems for the plans of others? For example, the Sharing Excellence project involved the release of staff from some teaching duties, which needed careful planning. Timetables are usually drawn up months in advance, and the people responsible will need to know about the project as far ahead as possible to help them to plan for it. This means involving the manager of the department and other key staff. Part-time replacements may not always be a possibility, so alternatives need to be thought about. What about extra administrative support, or additional resources for the course team to use as appropriate?

In your project plan you need to build in this time factor for prior planning and involve others beyond the project team in the negotiations. It is no good suddenly finding you have been successful with the bid, only to find members of staff cannot be released. For example, in year two of our project, additional departments were coming on stream. Half-way through year one I met with each of these 'new' heads of department to brief him on the project and to ask who might be an appropriate coordinator for the staff. I also involved the person responsible for timetabling in order to ensure that the coordinators could be released from teaching for one day per week. This early involvement of the heads of department helped to engage them in the project and gave them an opportunity to ask any questions and to discuss the benefits that were already starting to occur. At the start of the second academic year these coordinators were already in place and briefed. In fact we involved them in some meetings towards the end of year one, as we were keen to ensure they felt part of the team. Formal agreements were never drawn up, but we provided the coordinators with informal job descriptions describing what they were expected to do, which were based on the job description drawn up prior to interviewing the student coordinator. This proved to be really useful. If you are dividing tasks between different departments or different institutions, drawing up job or task specifications can be very helpful. It is likely to lead to fewer disagreements and gives all sides a better understanding of what is required.

Another consideration is the appointment of additional or external staff, for whom you will need to advertise. You will need to check the procedures for recruiting new staff in your institution. Devising job descriptions, advertising and then appointing can easily take up to six months. If you have not built this into your planning process, the project start could well be delayed by months, setting everything behind schedule. All these issues need careful planning to ensure that the project gets off to a flying start.

As mentioned earlier, we decided to appoint a recent graduate to work with the students at gathering feedback and seeking their views on what they saw as making effective lecturers. This was to be a new appointment and the only external appointment to the project. The project manager drew up a draft job description, which was circulated for comments and modified appropriately, so that as soon as funding was secured we were ready to advertise. The interview team included the original group members, in order to involve them again in the process. For some staff this was the first time they had been involved in an interview process, and it turned out to be a very positive learning experience.

This involvement of staff highlighted the value of supporting the professional development of the project team by allocating some funding to staff development. While attendance at taught programmes, courses and workshops has a role to play in developing the capacity of individuals to perform more effectively in work contexts, they are not, and cannot be, the sole ingredients of effective continuing professional development provision. Gibbs, Blackmore and Shrives (1999) draw attention to the fact that staff are often unable to introduce change simply because the structural changes are controlled by people who are not present. Staff development does not always mean sending someone on a formal course or conference, as there are many ways in which staff can be developed. For example, this could include work shadowing, writing in small groups, mentoring, or structured 'fact-finding' visits. Inviting external speakers to the group to talk about their work helped to develop self-knowledge among team members. Also, presenting our work to them developed the self-confidence of team members and helped us to reflect on progress.

Regular team meetings were deliberately built into the life of the project. The function of these was to keep the project on track, to learn from each other and reflect on progress, and to develop the team professionally. During the first year of the project these days became increasingly difficult to organize due to prior teaching commitments. In the second year we decided we would always meet on a Tuesday. This information was successfully fed into the timetablers' planning framework, and this is a mechanism I would strongly suggest to others. Done sufficiently early, it makes the organization of the project easier to achieve.

STAGE FIVE: UNDERSTAND AND APPLY THE MANAGEMENT OF CHANGE

In understanding how your project may be successful it is useful to understand how change is managed. All too often at the end of a project staff move on, the material produced stays on the shelf, and many years later someone asks 'What happened to that project?' So it is worth spending time thinking about what change you would like to see once the project is completed and how any outcomes might be sustained. It might not necessarily be that the project continues. It might be that you wish to sustain a change in culture and climate, for example, where high-quality learning and teaching are valued.

A number of educational researchers have identified factors that are essential to the success of institutional change in learning and teaching. Key factors include leadership commitment, departmental climate, information links and interpersonal links. Hawkins and Winter (1997) identified five essential change processes that provide the link between operation and strategy:

- action;
- communication;
- ownership;
- reflection;
- nurture.

They refer to these as the ACORN model. Certainly these five change processes influenced our thinking and helped us to think about how we wanted certain changes to be managed. Each process can be taken in turn and applied to the Sharing Excellence project.

Action

If action is where change begins, it follows that the calibre of those taking the action will be critical to successful change. Our model of faculty coordinators was extremely successful, as flexibility and ownership at the local level proved to be essential. However, a key factor is the selection of appropriate people. In our case we wanted staff who would be respected by their departmental colleagues, who were interested in the learning and teaching process and wanted to be involved with the project and its development, and who were team players. That does not mean everyone has to be alike; in fact different styles within a team can help the project to develop. A few 'awkward' questions posed in the right way can be extremely helpful to the development of the project. Although the heads of department were responsible for selecting those staff, you can help to influence this process by setting out the kind of skills you require, and discussing with the department head who might be suitable. If you are dealing with other universities it may be that you have personal contacts or could arrange to meet with the head of department to discuss the project.

The good practice identified at this small group level was passed to departmental and faculty level. After the observations had taken place, the faculty coordinators organized events to discuss themes and issues that needed to be addressed. A number also held faculty 'Good Practice Days'. A very successful whole-university Learning and Teaching Conference acted as a main focus for staff across the university to meet together and share experiences. Key aims of this approach were to encourage the enthusiasts and nurture the successes. The outcomes of this action were the identification and dissemination of good practice. In addition, teamwork was strengthened, collaboration became more evident, and case studies and videos of good practice were produced.

Communication

It is important that a high profile is established early on. The higher education institution(s) and the higher education community in general need to know what is happening. This can be achieved at a variety of levels. Within each institution or group of institutions fliers can be produced, details put in the institutional newsletter, or information given to the appropriate Subject Centre within the Learning and Teaching Support Network. A Web site set up quickly can give project details and expected outcomes. With the Sharing Excellence project, presentations were made internally to key network groups, including senior managers and course leaders, while within each department the faculty coordinator disseminated information. First, we produced two newsletters per year (called *TALK*) and, second, a journal (called *Innovation*) which contained longer articles on effective practice. These publications were good vehicles for disseminating outcomes as well as encouraging staff to write about their practice. At university level a steering group of senior mangers enabled the upward flow of information. Externally, communication was achieved through conference presentations and publications, with a Web site disseminating the material internationally.

Ownership

Developing support both top-down and bottom-up encourages ownership. At the local level (bottom-up), each faculty coordinator was responsible for between 20 and 65 staff. To ensure top-down support we involved senior managers in a steering group that was chaired by the Deputy Vice Chancellor. It included deans, heads of department, the external evaluator and faculty coordinators. These lines of communication were essential to the success of the project. (The role of the Steering Group is discussed in Chapter 4.)

Reflection (and also evaluation)

Hawkins and Winter (1997: 36) highlight the fact that reflection is far from instinctive, that it needs building into agendas and that it is required in reports. Evaluation when used in a formative and summative way enriches project development and increases efficiency and effectiveness. Leaving evaluation until the end of a project allows little room for formative feedback to influence modifications required. We were keen to develop an evaluation strategy early in the project to enable formative feedback to occur. In the Sharing Excellence project the internal and external evaluators performed different but complementary roles. The internal evaluator focused on staff and outcomes at the departmental level and at the level of programme management. Questionnaires were analysed, focus groups set up and staff interviewed. The external evaluator concentrated on senior managers. One-to-one meetings were conducted as well as focus group meetings. This helped to raise awareness of strategic issues relating to the management of organizational change.

Nurture

Hawkins and Winter (1997) advise not leaving this to the last minute for, as they state, 'An innovation will only outlive the enthusiasts if lasting systems and structures support it' (p 40).

The essential challenge for the Sharing Excellence project was to move from successful practice to a state where new methods have deep roots within the institution. This meant that the innovations needed to be incorporated into institutional systems and structures. Marginal activity needs to be brought into the mainstream of university life. Two of the most successful outcomes of the project were a Centre for Learning and

Teaching (CeLT), and the appointment at senior level of nine faculty learning and teaching coordinators. The first major task of the new centre was to produce a learning and teaching strategy for the university. The Sharing Excellence project enabled the university to focus on the future direction of learning and teaching, with the following key questions being addressed:

- What are the key learning and teaching issues for the university?

- What support is available to fund and manage these projects?

- How do we spread good practice?

- Do we know what we are doing across the university?

- Is the learning and teaching strategy working effectively?

- Are we being efficient and effective or are we just being busy?

Outputs included case study material, videos of staff and students, a staff resource pack on student feedback, a teaching portfolio, conference presentations, articles, and a Web site. A new learning and teaching development fund was set up by the Deputy Vice Chancellor to encourage innovations in learning and teaching. These developments led to a culture shift, with more deans and heads of department acknowledging and supporting issues relating to learning and teaching.

Although a great deal was learnt from the project, incorporating effective change is an ongoing process that requires institutional support. One of the key learning points illustrated by this chapter is that a well-planned project – with clear outcomes, milestones, and with an evaluation and dissemination strategy – facilitates an immediate and effective start to the project.

REFERENCES

Gibbs, G, Blackmore, P and Shrives, L (1999) *Supporting Staff Development within Departments*, Oxford Centre for Staff Development, Oxford

Hawkins, P and Winter, J (1997) *Mastering Change: Learning the lessons of Enterprise in Higher Education Initiative*, Department for Education and Employment, Sheffield

EDITORS' COMMENTARY

Brenda Smith stresses above all the importance of clear planning and development at the outset of a project. Several other FDTL projects cast further light on this.

The project Brenda Smith describes took place wholly in one institution. The LUMEN project (Leeds University Music Education iNitiative), although based at Leeds University and not involving a formal consortium, was set up to work very closely with a Network Group of 14 further and higher education institutions. This fact alone required the LUMEN project manager to take a very different approach to planning. A major contributor to the success of LUMEN was the Network Group's buying into the LUMEN plans at an early stage. How did LUMEN achieve this? The LUMEN project manager had been instrumental in a DfEE-funded project that had succeeded in reviving the music discipline network, via a consultative process and a conference. Two factors – building on the network, and the emergence of a sense of a community of practice – were important in the early planning stages of LUMEN. A key learning point from the earlier DfEE project was the importance of a forum for discussing and sharing ideas and concerns about both subject-specific and generic developments in learning and teaching. This, together with the need to encourage and enhance a sense of ownership of the development process among academic colleagues, prompted the inclusion of a clearly defined and consistent consultative strand from the outset of LUMEN.

As part of the planning process for Sharing Excellence at Nottingham Trent University (in order to secure additional funding for work in all the faculties), Brenda Smith enlisted the support of senior managers before the project began and continued that relationship throughout the project. In FDTL Phase Three, the Keynote Project – a consortium of Nottingham Trent University, the London Institute and the University of Leeds – also enlisted the early support of a dean who had a leading national role in art and design education. Enlisting the support of a senior member of the university and of the discipline was just one idea that David Allen, the project manager of the Keynote Project, brought from his work as a member of the project team on Sharing Excellence. David's role in transferring this latter project and its practices to the University of Kent at Canterbury may have enabled him to reflect on the particular strengths of project management in Sharing Excellence, and to apply them to the Keynote Project.

By contrast, in FDTL Phase Three, the GLAADH (Globalizing Art, Architecture and Design History) project, a very solid plan was developed through discussion between senior members of the three consortium institutions – the Open University, Sussex University and Middlesex University

– and then implemented by a project manager recruited to run the project. This presented a very different challenge for the project planners. They needed to build commitment within their institutions, but in a way that still allowed space to the incoming project manager to make it her own. This required an approach recommended by Rosabeth Moss Kanter (2001) of being tight on goals, but looser on the detail of implementation. The three architects of the project continued their involvement with the project as members of the Steering Group, supporting the project manager carrying out their goals.

Many projects discover that, however well formulated their initial plans, major changes are required as the project unfolds. For more on adapting to change during a project see Chapter 6 by June Balshaw and Howard Senter.

Failure to have a clear plan, with allocated times and responsible people, can allow a project to drift along, with project members aware that the rate of progress is not great but unaware of just how far the project is slipping. In this way, ultimate completion of the project can be put in jeopardy from a very early stage. If the only milestones are the delivery of annual and final reports, and two workshops along the way, then progress cannot be usefully monitored. Loose planning also makes the appointment of staff problematic, because it is difficult to write satisfactory project job descriptions. More broadly, failure to quantify time and responsibility often means that the project team has not grasped the reality of their task and what it entails.

REFERENCE

Kanter, R M (2001) speaking in *They Did it Their Way*, Video 3 for Open University MBA Course B822, Creativity, Innovation and Change

3

Networking

Sally Fincher

Networking is a fundamental – if seldom formalized – activity for staff and educational development. Much of the work of a staff and educational developer is to assist in the process of growth and change in individuals. Some of the constituent activities which help to achieve this aim – sharing ideas, disseminating knowledge, building to mutual advantage – are all features of networks and networking. For educational development in general, and for funded educational development projects in particular, networking has a significant role to play in achieving maximum impact.

EFFECTIVE NETWORKING

Networking is also a natural human activity, and the ways in which a network is activated and sustained are commonplace. There is nothing unusual in talking with like-minded people about common interests, or in chatting with colleagues over coffee, or in attending a meeting on a burning issue, or in joining a professional association. And it is important to recognize that many of the mechanisms used in informal exchanges like this are often modelled within the formal arena, by virtue of their familiarity.

Within educational development projects, however, we are engaged in more formal, intentional activity: for example, the deliberate promulgation of specific information which the originators take to be useful to a specific, intended audience. Conscious awareness of networking makes it more effective. Explicit networking activity should:

● clearly identify the target community and the benefits that they wish to accrue (and are willing to pay for, in time or money);

- be founded on a strong conceptual model of what the network, or networking activity, is to achieve; and

- utilize appropriate networking modes to realize the desired aims.

I believe these three interrelated characterizations of deliberate networking to be vital. I believe it because of several years of (sometimes bitter) experience in trying to create and sustain networks, and in coming up (sometimes forcibly) against other people's assumptions of what networks are and what networking is trying to achieve. I am, by inclination and occupation, an academic. So, when I first encountered this disparity of interpretation of networks and networking, I studied the disparity with the intention of trying to capture and characterize the essential, underlying features that constituted this thing called networking in its various manifestations. I succeeded in doing this (at least to my own satisfaction). This chapter is a summary of what I found.[1]

TARGET COMMUNITIES AND NETWORKING MODES

There seem to be two fundamental forms of network, which crucially depend on whether the word is interpreted as a noun or a verb. Think about it for a minute. Are you doing something when you are networking? Are you an active participant in the process? If so, the network is probably verb based. On the other hand, are you joining something when you are networking? Are you taking advantage of activities that are organized on the members' behalf? If so, the network is probably noun based.[2]

A verb network advantages its members by their contact with each other. Its value resides in the inherent skills of its members, and the interactions between members, not in any formal package of benefits. The archetype of a verb-based network is the Gentleman's Club: joining such a network buys members nothing except proximity to others. Individuals can only benefit from the opportunities that membership offers by virtue of their own skills and interests. The cost of joining a verb-based network is quite high, in that the people who join will be expected to put in quite a lot of effort over quite a long time.

A noun network has an identity, and value, separate from any given member or selection of members. The most obvious clue to whether a network is noun based lies in whether it is something to which people can belong. You cannot, in any sensible way, belong to an activity, so if you belong to a network there must be something external to the individual activity of the members. The archetypal example here is a trades union, which works to create things for the benefit of members that they cannot achieve through their own skills and interests alone. A member can join, and receive the benefits of membership, with no expectation of additional commitment or further interaction. It is quite cheap for members to participate in a noun-based network.

I felt happier when I had captured this distinction. It made sense of some of the ambiguity I had found in other people's usage of the word network. It also made sense in terms of creating a network: it gave me a way to construct appropriate activities depending on what I wanted to achieve.

NETWORK MODELS

While my verb/noun distinction was satisfying, it did not fully explain what I saw. With this conceptual tool, I could now look at other people's networking activity and say 'Oh yes, they're using a verb mode', or sometimes 'Oh dear, they're trying to use a verb mode but they're employing noun-type activities. That won't work very well.' Which was well and good. But it was not enough to explain the diversity of forms that I saw. I had gone some way towards saying what people were doing, but not why they were doing it.[3]

So I analysed the characteristics of a set of 24 DfEE-funded discipline networks. This set was a good target for several reasons. First, I was running one of these networks, so I was intimately interested in their success. Second, they were all engaged in staff and educational development. Third, although superficially engaged in the same activity (across different disciplines), they displayed widely different forms. I characterized their network models in three ways:

- by whether they were using verb or noun activities;

- by the audience they were trying to influence (either a complete constituency – for example 'all theology lecturers in the UK'; or a subset of a constituency – for example 'all theology lecturers interested in using Problem Based Learning'); and

- by a description of their purpose.

For convenience, I also gave each type of network a name (see Table 3.1).[4]

Table 3.1

Mode	Audience	Characterization of purpose	Name
Verb	Subset	A network that focuses on *creating opportunities* for individuals to do things primarily for their own individual development. (For instance, a network based around a series of skills-based workshops.)	Opportunist
	Subset	A network that is formed around the personal vision, energy and contacts of the organizer. These leaders are characterized by their *subject expertise* (which gains them academic credibility and the respect of their peers), their *length of time within their disciplinary area* (which gives them a large number of contacts), and their *enthusiasm.*	Charismatic
Noun	Complete constituency	A network that *adds onto* the results of one or more previous initiatives, accreting experience and membership from that.	Accretor
	Complete constituency	A network that shares the same vision as Accretors, but which *starts from square one.* There is no previous activity (or none visible to the organizers) to use as a foundation.	Builder
Functional[5]	Subset	A network that focuses on a *single aspect* of staff or educational development. (In staff and educational development terms these are often student centred rather than staff centred and defined with a more limited scope and lifetime.)	Problem solver
	Either a subset or a complete constituency	A network that views a network as having a centre to which everything refers. These centres are sometimes distinguished by being a different *type* of organization from the network members (so many universities are served by one professional association), and sometimes by *providing something* that none of the network members have, but all want (so, many branch libraries and one copyright library).	Radial

ACTUALIZING A NETWORK: PROJECT EPCOS

At the start of the FDTL funding initiative, I had all these ideas in my head. Let me tell you the story of how I applied them in a practical situation. This is the story of the Effective Projectwork in Computer Science (EPCOS) project, which was funded under Phase One of the FDTL initiative (£250,000 over three years).

Networking zero: building

I previously ran the Computer Science Discipline Network (CSDN), one of 24 discipline networks funded by the then Department for Education and Employment. It was funded for two years but lasted, under its own momentum, for a further three. The aim of CSDN, indeed of all the discipline networks, was 'to promote and disseminate good practice in teaching and learning of Computer Science' (or any other named discipline). I was employed from the start as project manager. At that time, I knew very few people outside my own institution, and could name no one who was specifically interested in the teaching and learning aspects of Computer Science. My first (and continuing) task was to 'form a network'.

The first thing I did was to assume that there was an interest in the area and that there was an associated need for information, sharing and discussion of these issues. From that basis we established mechanisms to encourage this activity: a Web site containing useful resources and a mailing list to carry discussion. We timetabled a series of events: one-day workshops and a larger conference. This activity was fine as far as it went, but it needed people – the nodes in the network – to make it work. We found these in two ways. One way was by a blanket of advertising. We sent out paper flyers, announcements to e-mail lists, and had inserts put into conference packs. The second way required more effort, but ultimately was more successful. It so happened that at the time I was travelling around the country for another purpose. At every university I visited (and at every town I was passing through and had the time to stop) I cold-called the Computing department. I would phone or e-mail ahead to try to identify the best person to talk to (usually this was the Head of Teaching and Learning) and then ask for a short meeting a few days hence. Although greeted with greater or lesser enthusiasm, this request was never refused. After several months of these occasional visits, I could name a person (and put a face to the name) in almost every Computing department in the UK who had at least heard of CSDN. I could target them for further advertising, but also took care to try to broker their interests – that is to say, if I knew someone was interested in plagiarism issues, I would pass on any new information I discovered about that – giving them extra value from the network and an incentive to keep it in their mind.

Why did this work? This modelled a classic noun network. There was very little required of network members to receive benefits – they just came to events, used the Web site, and read (and maybe posted to) the mailing list. Yet there was 'a sort of sense of community'[6] which provided a good cost–benefit trade-off for participants.

Where did this fail? The network building depended exclusively on my efforts. The funding was way too little (a half-time post for two years) and over too short a period for the stated ambitions of the initiative (which was to establish self-funding, self-continuing networks). The only thing possible was to establish an awareness of the need and a prototype solution.

Good and bad was that the network was so strongly identified with a single personality. If members did not like the central person, then they were much less likely to value the aims and products of the network. Equally, if I stopped pushing there was no one to take over.

Networking one: accreting (for a purpose)

More or less exactly at the end of the CSDN funding period, the FDTL initiative was launched. By this time, we were well positioned to make a bid. I already knew (had come to know) the interested and motivated people in the area, and I looked to create a small, effective, focused network out of them. We targeted people to form a bidding consortium and made the invitation at an existing event, by hosting a dinner the night before the CSDN conference, to discuss future possibilities. Of those present that evening, only one took no further part in the proceedings. Neither at this meeting, nor at the subsequent one, was there any discussion of the subject of the bid (which eventually proved to be project work in Computer Science). This was not to be a noun based network where people were getting benefit simply for belonging – for paying their fees – but a verb-based one. It was built on the participants, their interests and their capacities. What we were going to do together emerged from that.

Why did this work? This built on the established interests of the members, their individual reputations, and that of CSDN. Mostly, there was a recognition of the benefits of working with each other.

Where did this fail? It absolutely required a verb-based mode of networking. Members did not necessarily know – from the expectations that the previous noun-based mode of CSDN had given them – what they were signing up for.

Networking two: internal functional network

Once the EPCOS consortium network was established, a bid made and funding won, internally it became a functional network, with explicit goals over a limited lifetime. Each consortium partner was required to:

- deliver one workshop (thus ensuring that there would be ten workshops over three years in geographically diverse locations);

- attend regular meetings; and

- adopt a piece of teaching practice from another institution and transfer a piece of their own teaching practice elsewhere.

Why did this work? There were clear and equal aims which each consortium member had to achieve. Ownership of outcomes and deliverables was distributed across all members.

Where did this fail? Not everyone could make the transition to verb-based mode, and its requirements on participation. There were three kinds of failure:

- Perception of value: some project members did not get enough benefit from the network to contribute to the work. Their institutions did not value the kind of activity that EPCOS represented (counting neither for teaching nor research). If the activity was not going to help the staff involved within their home institution, there was no incentive to participate. This was manifest by one institution which dropped out of the EPCOS network.

- Failure of expectation: verb-mode networks depend on the quality of the members. Not all institutions expected the high level of commitment that EPCOS demanded; and not all members of the EPCOS network contributed equally. This created problems for other network members who resented carrying passengers.

- Failure of support: some institutions seconded high-value staff, but did not internally value or reward that individual's work in this area. For example, they did not adjust the load of the staff members to allow time for EPCOS activity, or did not allocate funds and resources to support their participation. This was manifest in our losing a member of the EPCOS network, even though their institution still apparently valued the association.

Networking three: building (again)

To achieve the aims of EPCOS (which, in summary, were to advance the effective use of projects in computer science education) we had to involve a community from outside the consortium. In this we returned to a noun-based model, leveraging other networks. We sent advertising and mailings out via CSDN and the (then) CTI Centre for Computing.[7] Once individuals had requested information, or attended a workshop, they continued to receive information on our activities and copies of the materials we produced unless (and until) they asked us to stop. Thus, there was no expectation of contribution, just the benefit of receiving the materials. Interestingly, although the distributed model mitigated against it, EPCOS events did accrue some workshop regulars, people who would travel the country to attend more than one, creating a kind of penumbral second circle network that we had not anticipated.

Why did this work? The distinctiveness of some of the dissemination products (notably the Atlas)[8] created a visible 'brand image' – non-EPCOS network members had a way of recognizing each other, and had an immediate point of contact. Just seeing one of our posters on an office wall would stimulate discussion, 'Oh, did you get one of those, too?'

Where did this fail? Because the primary focus of the consortium members was on the work that was being undertaken, on the interactions with each other to a specific end, it was sometimes hard to see beyond the verb-based mode to the outside community. Because of the regular (and sometimes intense) meetings, a shorthand vocabulary for the work emerged and was used with increasing frequency within the consortium. When we talked with people outside the EPCOS network, we used the same vocabulary, which, we discovered, was opaque outside the environment in which the vocabulary originated. This may sometimes have led to a feeling that it was not worth trying to bring 'outsiders' up to speed, and that our internal network was more important than the larger community.

In terms of networks and networking, one of the most interesting things I learnt from EPCOS was that, unlike the networking models I found within the discipline networks initiative, there was no one single networking model or mode here. From my previous understanding, a more fluid model had emerged, where different constructs were used to suit different purposes and personnel, and these changed over the life of the project.

SUMMARY

So this is the EPCOS story. It's just the way I did it. It's one story among many, a single possible model of the ideas of networks and networking. There are many other stories, many other ways in which this could have been accomplished. But this way was pretty successful, and I think its success was due to conscious reflection on the structures of, and uses of, network models. And it leads me to believe that an awareness of the ways in which networks are manifest, and the activities that encourage and develop them, are very useful implements in the toolbox of the project manager.

NOTES

1 For a full write-up, see University of Kent at Canterbury Computing Laboratory Technical Report no 7–01.
2 This interpretation may not be explicit in the minds of the organizers/members, but can be seen from the type(s) of activity and rhetoric that the network employs.
3 And both of these questions leave out the 'how'. But it seems that 'how' is pretty obvious – it is the usual mechanisms of newsletters, mailing lists, workshops, conferences, etc.
4 When I identified these models, it seemed that a network was either one thing or another, that it had a single aim and constructed its work to fit that. However, the discipline networks were a very short-lived initiative (most had existence for only one or two years) and it seems likely that these models were actually 'snapshots' at stages of development, and that a more prolonged networking activity might pass through several stages and modes.
5 I captured the additional mode 'functional', as some networks were driven by an aim that relied on the way they viewed their function within their community, and this was a defining characteristic of their activity.
6 Quoted from the CSDN first year evaluator's report.
7 The Computers in Teaching Initiative (CTI) Centre for Computing is now the Learning and Teaching Support Network Centre for Information and Computer Sciences.
8 The 'Atlas' was a poster-sized compilation of our survey results. We used a professional graphic designer, so it was eye-catching and attractive. We called it the Atlas, because it provided an overview of the terrain we were mapping.

EDITORS' COMMENTARY

Sally Fincher describes the growth of networking from the discipline network in Computer Science. But how can projects build in existing cooperative practice in the absence of such a discipline network? The FDTL Phase 3 project Better Together based at Sheffield Hallam University identified the need to network across various disciplines in the built environment. The project required surveyors, planning officers, housing managers, architects and civil engineers to work inter-professionally to provide an educational framework within which students could develop the abilities to work in the increasingly collaborative way that is becoming characteristic (under government prompting) of urban development. Methods included engaging with all the relevant professional institutions, working with the LTSN Subject Centre and embracing research into inter-professional education in other subject areas.

Another example of networking, also from the world of the built environment, is provided by the Learning to Work: Working to Learn project at Kingston University. Again, the project manager has targeted professional bodies, this time to support the development of postgraduate qualifications gained through work-based learning. One fascinating issue raised by this networking has been the development of a coherent approach to the assessment of workplace learning by mentors outside higher education and from different professions.

One approach to networking for dissemination, developed by the LUMEN Project Manager (see also the commentary to Chapter 2), is a 'fan-shaped' networking strategy. This involves a core layer of, say, four partners across which the project has a relatively strong focus of attention and investment of resources. The next layer involves perhaps six or eight departments or institutions, and the next layer 10, with each successive layer having a less intensive relationship with the project team.

This strategy is likely to be of most use where the intention is to pilot a product or process across several departments or institutions, and where it may be useful to have different kinds of involvement secured from different kinds of institution. The first layer may well develop the product, the next layer will pilot and feedback horizontally and vertically to the first-layer institutions, and the next layer will pilot and adapt, often with help and support from the first two layers. The advantages include a ready-made feedback chain, a sense of shared development, a greater likelihood of adaptation and implementation, and a wider range of paradigms of adaptation and use by the people for whom it was originally designed, so enhancing further the implementation and embedding of the project outcomes. This kind of approach may also help to reinforce a sense of a community of practice, of working collaboratively on a common problem or issue.

4

Making good use of a steering committee

Angela Smallwood

THE NEED FOR A STEERING COMMITTEE

To take on running one of the first FDTL projects in 1996 was to walk into a new and highly complex world. Projects have been defined by one commentator as being essentially about 'demands for change in areas of complexity' (Andersen, Grude and Hang, 1995: 173). The project I was heading was further complicated because it was not confined to a single institution: it involved a newly formed consortium of five autonomous universities in taking up a generic teaching initiative, co-customizing it and then disseminating it further still across the higher education (HE) sector. This move to override institutional autonomy was replicated within each of the partner universities, where a subject-based pilot was to be followed by the dissemination of the initiative from the pilot department to other disciplines, all with their own traditions of autonomy. Furthermore, the consortium was diverse in nature, involving three pre-1992 universities and two 1992 universities. This diversity was built in deliberately, with a view to broadening the relevance of the project outcomes for the sector as a whole. Clearly a steering committee was required. In addition to the necessity of having an evidently responsible, representative and informed group to oversee the proper use of a large sum of public money, there was the need to gain regular overviews of activities across the five universities and to coordinate the outcomes.

When first drafting the bid with colleagues, I assumed that the steering group would be a monitoring and guiding body, and I remember hoping that, in practice, ways would somehow be found to turn it into something more participatory than a mere report-receiving group, or talking shop. In retrospect I can now see that it was a good deal different from that, in ways I could not have imagined. It had an integral role among other inter-institutional groupings that came into being during the project, to make the consortium work well, and made a steady and essential contribution to the three-year process of maximizing the project's achievements.

The most familiar functions of steering committees would commonly include some or all of the following:

- giving representation to stakeholders;

- sharing knowledge and expertise;

- providing guidance on priorities and problems;

- approving plans, budgets and reports;

- giving support;

- monitoring progress;

- steering reactions to change;

- monitoring quality of implementation;

- acknowledging success;

- boosting the morale of the project team.[1]

The steering committee for Personal and Academic Development for Students in Higher Education (PADSHE) certainly did all of these. However, the thinking behind its constitution began not with the standard remit but with an attempt to address the central problem of how to run a consortium-based project well: the specifying of a formal support structure for the project work in each of the five universities in the consortium in order to maximize the likelihood of successful outcomes at each site.

As PADSHE involved a good deal of change management, its implementation would not have been easy anywhere. The project bid was based on an innovative scheme, in English Studies at the University of Nottingham, to quality assure personal tutoring. It had been identified as good practice by the Teaching Quality Assessment exercise in 1994 because it had transformed patchy, reactive pastoral tutoring into academic-led, proactive, equal-entitlement provision, documented in Personal and Academic Records (PARs). PARs had also formed the basis of a supported system of personal development planning for undergraduates and had drawn in virtually 100 per cent student participation. The consortium members were to relate the PADSHE concept to their specific needs and contexts, develop pilot schemes in English and then disseminate further. With this crucial acknowledgement of the differences between institutions came, inevitably, an apparent reinforcement of the principle of institutional autonomy, which made it difficult to see how far work within any individual partner university could, in the interests of the project as a whole, be directed from the outside.

Direction was definitely needed, because the approach was new and the consortium had been put together in some haste, partly opportunistically, with the result that only two of the English departments had any previous experience of recording achievement in HE. Inasmuch as I had any authority as project director, it was limited to my being perceived as the inventor of PADSHE and the team member with the most experience of the teaching development. In terms of university hierarchies, I was a senior lecturer, contemplating the direction of the work of seconded fellow academics who were (in some cases) professors, and (in all cases) nominated by their own institutions and wholly new to me.[2] All the partner institutions acknowledged a prior wish to make changes in the area of teaching development central to the project, but the team members who were put forward started out with different levels of understanding of it, and represented a diversity of positions in terms of professional status and access to senior management. How valuable an opportunity was the task of constructing and running the steering committee, in terms of promoting the overall aims of the project?

THE RELATIONSHIP BETWEEN THE STEERING COMMITTEE AND THE PROJECT PARTNERS: ISSUES OF AUTHORITY, AUTONOMY AND ENGAGEMENT

The first move was to use the project bid document (which later took on the status of a contract) to define in each partner university – and specifically for each team leader – a support structure that would maximize the chances of successful internal dissemination. As Nottingham had already begun to introduce PADSHE to disciplines other than English, the Nottingham arrangements, built with the guidance of the academic manager of our Enterprise in Higher Education project and our Director of Teaching Enhancement, were mirrored in the other four universities. Each was to have an internal steering group whose membership would both reach high up the hierarchy of the university and also have the breadth to ensure that developments would be appropriate across the institution.

As Figure 4.1 shows, the core of the formal support structure was a team of three:

● the academic project leader in English Studies;
● the senior manager (often Pro-Vice-Chancellor for Teaching, or equivalent); and

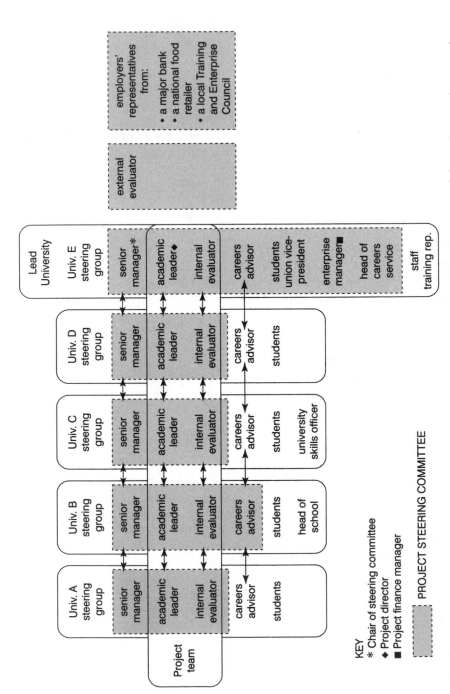

Figure 4.1 *The relationship between individual institutions' steering groups, the project team and the project steering committee*

KEY
* Chair of steering committee
♦ Project director
■ Project finance manager

⬜ PROJECT STEERING COMMITTEE

● the internal evaluator (with a formative, developmental role) who was either an educationalist or another academic based in a discipline other than English.

The stipulation that the team leader be an academic was made following the success at Nottingham of seconding research-active academics to the Teaching Enhancement Office on a part-time basis to lead teaching innovations. The commitment of a senior manager gave the team two-way contact with institutional policy making. In practice, the senior manager's participation took a variety of forms in different institutions, from chairing the local steering group, through receiving progress reports at the appropriate university committee, to regular one-to-one update meetings with the team leader. The requirement that the evaluator should come from another discipline had two purposes: it provided an interlocutor for the team leader; and it opened an immediate route to dissemination outside English.

The three key figures in each university team (project leader, senior manager, internal evaluator) were given places on the PADSHE steering committee, not least in order to cement their grouping within their own institution. To signal the importance of senior management support I persuaded the Nottingham Pro-Vice-Chancellor (PVC) for Teaching to take the Chair of the steering committee, and one of his opposite numbers from a 1992 consortium university to accept the role of Vice-Chair. At the first meeting of the steering committee we allocated a slot of time to discussion in peer groups, bringing the PVCs together to exchange ideas about how they could support the project aims in their own institutions and in the sector. The establishment of this peer group proved especially useful at a point in mid-project when I needed to ask my senior manager to pick up the phone and speak to another PVC, in order to sort out a problem which had arisen. In meetings of the steering committee, the responsiveness within this group tended to bear out Andersen's observation of the dynamic of similar situations in business environments:

> When matters are discussed in a steering committee with several line managers, it is easier to get individual line managers to realize their responsibilities ... when they see that others also take on similar responsibilities.
>
> (Andersen, Grude and Hang, 1995: 180)

Given the demands on senior managers' time, full attendance could not be expected, but over the three years of the project each senior representative made about half the meetings. From the point of view of motivating senior managers to attend as much as they could, it was fortunate that the project sat obviously close to strategic issues, including student support and guidance (under scrutiny in external Subject Review) and the implementation of the recommendations of the Dearing Review of Higher Education (NCIHE, 1997), especially those on independent self-managed learning and lifelong learning.

It was understood that the steering groups in the individual universities would need to include further members, principally a representative of the university's careers advisory service – because issues of skills, employability and career development feature strongly within the concept of personal development planning – and some students. In practice, effective groups took shape in a variety of ways, adding sometimes a head of school, sometimes a colleague from a related project elsewhere in the university, who could provide expertise and take the role of critical friend.

Figure 4.1 shows the interrelationships between the central project team (carrying out the day-to-day work of the project), the project steering committee and the five steering groups in the consortium universities.

Although some were held at other times, most meetings of the project team were placed back-to-back with steering committee meetings on the same day, creating two opportunities rather than one while everyone was in the same place. Sometimes senior managers left after the steering committee meeting, sometimes they stayed on for the team meeting. But the existence of the team meeting later in the day made it easier to streamline the business of the steering committee and allow it to focus on its specific tasks, passing any detailed follow-up to the team.

However, just as it was useful in that first steering committee meeting to bring the senior managers together for peer group exchange, and just as it was obviously essential to convene team leaders and internal evaluators across the project on a regular basis, so, as time went on, it became clear that cross-project peer group work in further areas would be beneficial to promote progress, quality and cohesion across the consortium. Both actual and potential cross-project peer groups can be seen in Figure 4.1.

The most obvious figures to draw into such a group were the careers advisers, whose importance was recognized by the inclusion of two of them on the project steering committee. This idea gave rise to the PADSHE Careers Advisers' Forum, an annual day, the venue for which moved around the consortium, bringing together this set of key project players who would otherwise have been operating in isolation. As Figure 4.1 suggests, peer group conferencing cut across institutional autonomy effectively to achieve greater convergence by addressing just one or two layers within an institution at a time. (There is an analogy here perhaps with the operation of the FDTL itself and of the LTSN subject centres.)

And as Figure 4.1 further suggests, it would have been highly beneficial, on the same principle, to convene forums outside the steering committee for the staff developers in the five universities and, of course, for the students, but funding and time were already stretched and I simply did not think of it.

DIRECTING CROSS-CONSORTIUM ACHIEVEMENT

Figure 4.1 also shows that a group of members of the steering committee came from outside the consortium. The majority of these were employers' representatives, based in or near Nottingham, who generously made the time to attend most meetings. My original assumption was that their presence would give a 'real world' perspective on the employability agenda within personal development planning, and bring expertise and the authority of an end-user to the discussion of the processes and documentation being developed. This was indeed the case; but there was more. The employers brought useful contacts and valuable sample materials, including job application forms and staff development frameworks, but they also contributed a high level of interest and enthusiasm for the concept, which had a major impact on the mood and motivation of the rest of the committee. And in the debate between the fact of diversity within the consortium and the potential for standardization across the consortium, which rapidly became a theme in the development of the project, their plea for at least a standardized core for both process and product was influential.

The issue of diversity versus standardization operated on two quite different levels. First, in terms of the teaching development itself, we were committed to learning about the full range of needs across the sector and to creating space for the PADSHE concept to be fulfilled in a shared spirit, while being interpreted as variously as necessary, taking on board the different starting points within existing good practice that the five universities presented. A balance had to be struck: having explored the feasibility of identifying a common core, the steering committee eventually adopted a set of quality guidelines for use across the consortium. Second, in terms of project progress, however, the paramount need was to achieve standardization of achievement across the partner universities and to minimize diversity.

Here another external member of the steering committee – the External Evaluator – was particularly influential. Her remit was of course to take an overview across the whole project and to coordinate the evaluation work of the internal evaluators in the partner institutions. She had a clear practical need to standardize arrangements across the consortium to facilitate her assessing, synthesizing and reporting processes. In the event, the early agreement of the evaluation framework served not only her purposes, but also authoritatively re-articulated the project objectives and created a consensus about the nature and the timing of common project activities that each institution would need to undertake. Impressed by the effectiveness of this standardizing strategy, I was keen to extend the idea to the work of the steering committee itself, which became the key forum for approving a series of standard instruments used across the partner universities for organizing project activity (see Figure 4.2).

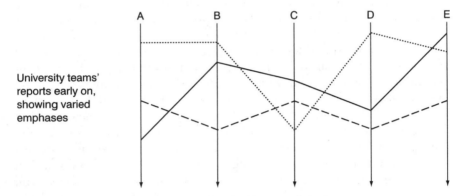

As the project developed, the steering committee increasingly introduced the use of pro forma-based reporting in order to achieve an element of standardization of project priorities across the consortium. Care was taken, however, even within the pro formas, to leave some unstructured free space to each institution for individual material.

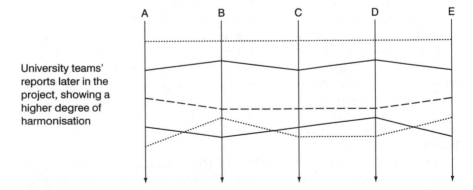

Figure 4.2   *An indication of how proformas enabled the steering committee to strengthen the focus on key cross-project issues increasingly as the project progressed*

The evaluation framework was agreed in a team meeting two months into the project. Following this, an evaluation pro forma for the first year was finalized at a steering committee, each university team undertaking to complete a copy. Further such pro formas, focusing on the specific project objectives for the second and third years, were considered at later meetings. There were also pro formas for activity plans submitted to the steering committee and for reports on the individual case studies that the different institutions developed in the third year. Another feature of the final year was the series of regional dissemination seminars, for which the steering committee approved a common format. This made for clarity and coherence when the series was publicized but also expressed a standard for the individual events, in terms of scope of content and level of institutional support. Each event was opened by a senior manager from the host institution and included a presentation, by the host university's team, on the PADSHE work in general and their case study in particular. It also drew in some employers, featured a modest exhibition about the whole project, and was used for internal as well as external dissemination.

The steering committee thus operated to authorize the use of standardized and standardizing structures and tools, which influenced the pace, quality and content of project activity inside the partner institutions. Given the consortium situation, this function of the PADSHE steering committee proved more sustained, further developed and more powerful than I had anticipated. The most obvious example of such a role was embodied in the provision that the steering committee would withhold the final 20 per cent of the project funding each year, pending the receipt of satisfactory progress reports from the partner institutions at the summer term meeting. This made the point particularly clearly, if crudely, that the steering committee was a lever to produce project performance. However, the more subtle means of consortium direction achieved by the steering committee and described above embodied the principle just as much.

A KEY ARENA OF PROJECT ACTIVITY

Performance was a key focus of the steering committee in at least two senses. There was performance in the sense of carrying out the project plan, and delivering the goods required by a series of deadlines. There were also other performances, however, in the form of presentations – public articulations of progress – which were equally essential to project success. At the start of the project, when I envisaged with a touch of dread that steering committee meetings might be dominated by tediously repetitive progress reports by the five academic team leaders, I had not fully appreciated the potential of this process. Not only did such regular reports enable the steering committee to identify and develop cross-project issues, as illustrated in Figure 4.2, they also constituted basic milestones along the project path for each partner, and provided a sequence of events against which project progress could be measured. In addition, each act of presentation articulated the results of an episode of learning for an individual team, and it clarified the presenter's position within the developing project, changing attitudes to the teaching initiative, and growing realization of its potential benefits and shortcomings for his or her own institution. In this respect, presentations to the steering committee constituted a semi-public performance which was a crucial half-way house between the private deliberations of the institutional steering groups and the final-year, public presentations made to the regional dissemination seminars, where, in practice, the institutional teams gave their clearest and most committed analyses of the project work.

This link between a core activity of the steering committee and a project activity carried out beyond it highlights what I have come to realize about the functioning of the consortium steering committee. Although I had feared it might be merely a talking shop, a peripheral ritual, a rubber stamp, I now see that it was itself the scene of key project actions, enacting the germ of each important activity, and that it gave status and authority to the areas of work that fanned out around it. Figure 4.3 represents this central role of the steering committee within the project as a whole in the form of the set of four rectangles in the middle of the diagram. The figure needs to be read from the centre outwards.

Each of the central rectangles represents an area of responsibility of the steering committee and is amplified by a larger box which has the same starting point but spreads out beyond it and represents the activities of the project team. The four areas of responsibility are mapped directly on to the make-up of the membership of the committee and the contents of its agendas. The top half of the diagram depicts activities involving the individual university teams: the objectives in focus here are (top left) the achievement of an effective compromise between institutional diversity and standardization, and (top right) the promotion of progress towards internal development and dissemination objectives in each institution. The bottom left-hand box shows cross-institutional activities, designed to achieve mutual exchange and coherence – if not convergence – of project outcomes across the consortium. In the bottom right-hand box we have cross-sector activities, directed towards maximizing the public impact of the project through national networking and external dissemination.

In many ways the project was very successful. The only specific target that the bid document had identified was in the area of internal dissemination: there was an objective to achieve the participation of 1,250 students across the consortium by the end of the second year. In the event, after three years, there were 8,000 students involved. External dissemination

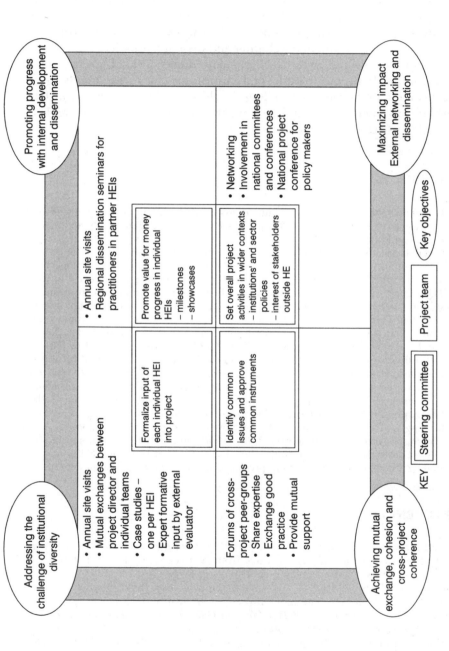

Figure 4.3 *The four key responsibilities of the steering committee, each amplified in areas of activity by the project team, in pursuit of key objectives shared by both the team and the committee*

also went very well, with the result that the project became recognized nationally as a resource for the sector and received further funding, as policy for the introduction of Progress Files in higher education continued to develop. The steering committee thus worked well in maximizing project achievement and in developing and disseminating its products and outcomes.[3] Meanwhile, in terms of its second major task, of working out a compromise between institutional autonomy and the needs of a consortium-based project in teaching development, it achieved as much as perhaps any such body could, among the first experiments in publicly funded cross-sector collaborations.

NOTES

1   Useful discussions of steering committees in business or higher education are found in Andersen, Grude and Hang (1995: 173–88); Barton and Temple (2000: 23); and Burton and Michael (1992: 37–38).
2   Given the relatively short lead time available for constructing the consortium prior to submitting the bid, the first partner was secured by approaching two of the subject assessors who had judged the Nottingham English PAR as good practice in their TQA report on the school. One was able to bring his school into the consortium. A second partner came through personal contact with the Head of School already recruited. The third partner was in an institution that had already made contact with Nottingham, in pursuit of follow-up information on the good practice identified in the TQA subject overview report for English. The fourth was invited to join the consortium in the interest of balance and as an institution with a good record for innovative teaching, which was conveniently located, close to one of the other institutions. A strikingly different approach to identifying project participants was operated by another FDTL Phase 1 project, History 2000, directed by Paul Hyland and Alan Booth, who invited departments to bid to join their project after having secured the funding, and who were, therefore, in a position to select their collaborators.
3   The organization of the project owed a great deal to advice received from Marjorie Allen, Carole Baume, Martin Binks, Mark Hadfield, Alan Howe and Sarah Turpin. Writing this chapter has made me appreciate even more the value of their experience.

REFERENCES

Andersen, E S, Grude, K V and Hang, T (1995) *Goal Directed Project Management: Effective techniques and strategies* (trans. from Norwegian by Roberta Wiig), 2nd edn, Coopers & Lybrand, Institute of Directors, Kogan Page, London

Barton, T and Temple, P (2000) *Milestones along the Critical Path: Project management in higher education*, Association of University Administrators, Manchester

Burton, C and Michael, N (1992) *A Practical Guide to Project Management: How to make it work in your organization*, Kogan Page, London

National Committee of Inquiry into Higher Education (NCIHE) (1997) *Higher Education in the Learning Society* (Report of the NCIHE), HMSO, London

EDITORS' COMMENTARY

The steering group which Angela Smallwood describes for the PADSHE Project was representative of all consortium members and contained a range of appropriate levels of staff including Pro-Vice-Chancellors and local evaluators.

The JEWELS Innovations project involved a collaboration between two universities: Exeter and Plymouth. Although the broad-based steering group had high-level representation in the form of two PVCs, it was run in an informal way and engaged participants in a variety of activities. One steering group activity focused on the problems that the project team were having with their Work Experience Award. The group of about 12 were divided into three subgroups and asked to come up with ideas on the following lines: 'How can we engage more students?', 'How can we offer greater added value?' and 'How can the award be funded?' After 20 minutes the subgroups fed back their suggestions to the team, which ended up with three flipcharts full of possible ideas and a continuing discussion. The activities secured real involvement by the steering group members and resulted in much constructive and useful feedback for the team.

Similarly, project RAPID, based at Loughborough University, used a large steering group. An observer of this steering group commented on the way in which participants seemed able to speak very freely even though the meeting was run formally. Many of the members were connected with the running of the project and had experience of the previous RAPID project, and the group were well informed, engaged and supportive of the project team.

In complete contrast the EPCOS steering group, the subject of Chapter 3, consisted of just three members who advised the project manager and project director throughout the project. The three members were one Vice-Chancellor and two Pro-Vice-Chancellors. Reflecting its membership, this steering group gave high-level strategic advice with strong emphasis on the project aligning itself with national initiatives and priorities. The steering group was unusual in many respects, one of which was that meetings often happened very early in the morning in London, before a national higher education meeting.

The LUMEN project, referred to in the commentaries on Chapters 2 and 3, strengthened the networking of its steering group by project team members paying personal visits to the institutions of the consortium members. During these visits they adopted the role of consultants on aspects of the development work of the project.

Problems with steering groups included: difficulties with recruiting members, sometimes resulting in insufficient diversity of viewpoint; high-level steering groups that were unwilling or unable to do substantive work;

steering groups perceived by the project manager as disabling because they directed and micro-managed, rather than steered; and under-informed steering groups that did not know enough about the project to offer useful advice and guidance.

5

Managing resources: the art of the possible

Tracey Varnava

INTRODUCTION

In common with other chapters in this book, the guidance that is offered here stems from my personal experience of project management. The context in which this experience has been gained is therefore important, and it is likely that some of the commentary will not exactly reflect your own situation. Even so, many of the insights offered here arise from an appreciation of the functioning of projects as organizations rather than from an insider's perspective on the foibles of a particular discipline area. It is therefore hoped that you will find what follows useful as you seek to achieve your project's aims and objectives within the university environment.

The chapter begins by briefly providing some contextual information on the National Centre for Legal Education (NCLE), the project that I managed between 1997 and 1999. This will help you to judge where there may be points of similarity, or not, between this project and your own. Against this you can consider the guidance and insight that is offered here on staffing, planning and managing a learning and teaching project. In a relatively short piece it is not possible to provide a step-by-step guide to each of these topics. However, the chapter aims to short-circuit the learning process by alerting you to problems, and possible solutions, which otherwise only tend to emerge in the light of experience.

THE PROJECT IN QUESTION

The NCLE project was a distinctive one within the canon of the Fund for the Development of Teaching and Learning (FDTL) for a number of reasons:

- It was a unitary centre serving all Higher Education institutions (HEIs) in the UK.

- Its purpose was to support and encourage effective learning and teaching practice wherever it appeared, and in whatever form it took.

- The NCLE was co-located with the Law Technology Centre (LTC) which already had a national profile built up over the best part of a decade, and had an established record for promoting innovative approaches to law teaching through the use of technology.

The NCLE project was designed to complement existing activity in law by focusing on generic, not just information and communication technology (ICT), approaches to supporting learning and teaching practice. As such it had a challenging brief. However, there was an expectation from those who devised the bid for NCLE that in-house experience of running the LTC, together with the ready availability of information resources such as mailing lists, would give the project a head start. Even so, because the two members of staff appointed to the project were not previously members of the law school, and therefore had no previous knowledge or experience of pre-existing resources or, indeed, how best to exploit them, the learning curve had a significantly steep gradient. As highlighted elsewhere in this book (see, for example, Chapters 2 and 7), the 'ownership' of the bid document is crucial, and where key project staff have not been involved in its genesis, thought needs to be given to familiarizing them with the thought processes of the bid architects. Project staff need to be able to subscribe to the aspirations of and the expectations for the project. Certainly, if you are a project manager and have not been involved in the bid writing process, you would be well advised to resist the urge to start working within the bid framework, to get things under way, until you have spent time exploring and understanding the issues that prompted the bid in the first place.

Despite the scale of NCLE activity, the project team (the coordinator, information officer and part-time director) managed over the three years of funding to achieve many of the original aims and objectives, and indeed instigated and promoted areas of activity that were not envisaged in the original bid for funding. This could only be achieved through the skills and abilities brought to the project by these three staff members and through the establishment of the robust organizational infrastructure that under-pinned the substantive work of the NCLE.

PEOPLE MAKE PROJECTS

With limited funds and wide remits, learning and teaching projects have to carefully balance staff budgets against the need to support core areas of activity. Some projects will choose to bring on board a spread of expertise by appointing staff on the basis of part-time contracts, often buying out the time of staff already in post inside or outside the host institution. Alternatively, as in the case of the NCLE, staff funds are used to appoint a small complement of full-time staff. There are pros and cons with either approach (see Table 5.1).

Table 5.1 *The staff/activity balance*

	Pros	*Cons*
Fewer staff but full-time	• Dedicated staff complement which gives a sense of cohesion and identity to the project	• Danger of becoming blinkered to other perspectives on managing the project and achieving its aims and objectives
	• Any areas of concern or interest can be quickly picked up and addressed by the manager	• Individual staff must take on a range of tasks and quickly develop the necessary skills
	• Accumulation of a core of management expertise available to the project	• Choosing the right people is key, getting it wrong can have serious consequences for the work of the project
More staff but part-time (often 'bought in')	• The project has access to a range of expertise in carrying out activities	• Difficulty of managing time: other demands will often impact on the time 'bought out' by the project. This will be hard for the project manager to address
	• The burden of achieving the aims and objectives of the project is shared	• Isolation and lack of engagement with the project
	• A wider pool of ideas for carrying out and developing the aims and objectives of the project	• Lack of 'team' effort – activity may become fractured

The drawbacks of each approach may or may not apply in individual cases, depending on the circumstances and the people involved. However, it is as well to be aware of the potential pitfalls. On whatever basis you choose to distribute the staffing budget – and it is possible that you will choose to appoint both full- and part-time staff – the project team will need to combine a range of skills and abilities. The smaller the team, the more adaptable, well organized and multi-skilled the individuals need to be.

The dream team

All learning and teaching projects have certain 'deliverables' and these tend to include events (workshops, seminars, conferences), Web pages, other electronic services such as jiscmail lists, newsletters, and other publications on substantive topics. How these tasks are divided between the members of the project team will depend on the number of appointments made and the abilities that each of the staff brings. However, to give you a taste of the range of skills that are required, Figure 5.1 is a job specification for the perfect project team member.

This is not meant to daunt you but to alert you to the type of abilities that you are going to need to recruit to make the project work. Again the relative importance of these abilities will vary according to circumstances. It is likely that you will always be missing some skills within the staff complement, the presence of which would make certain areas of project activity easier to achieve. In these circumstances, you will have to think creatively about how to fill these skill gaps. Options include: employing temporary staff; employing external consultants as required; devolving responsibility for the activity to existing groups/networks/experts. Of course, as highlighted in Table 5.1, the benefits of buying in additional expertise in whatever form have to be weighed against the additional resources required and the time taken in managing and coordinating part-time or off-site employees/agents of the project.

A recurring theme in teaching and learning projects is the ability of staff members to combine the 'academic' with the 'practical'. Project staff usually need to be self-servicing in terms of administration – dedicated administrative support may not be possible within the staff budget. They will also need to be flexible in their approach to their job description, particularly in a small team when it is often a case of filling in as required. It is likely that the full list of tasks, such as those listed in Figure 5.1, will need to broken down into their component parts and allocated to more than one person – hence the emphasis on team working. However, if a member of staff is able to see through a task on their own then, pragmatically, it makes sense to give them sole responsibility for that task, thus freeing up the time of other staff members.

The postholder will have responsibility for:

- developing, planning and organizing a learning and teaching events programme (up to six workshops, four seminars and one major national conference per year);
- designing, writing and publishing Web pages on the activities of the project;
- researching, cataloguing and developing a Web-based resource bank of materials;
- evaluating and reviewing educational learning technologies and their applicability to the subject area;
- compiling and editing a regular newsletter;
- providing a current awareness service via the Web pages;
- setting up and managing a range of electronic communication mechanisms;
- promoting and supporting the development of networks around interest areas;
- writing and presenting conference papers and workshop sessions on learning and teaching;
- designing and writing publicity material for the project;
- evaluating the progress of all areas of activity and reporting on a regular basis to the funding body and the project's advisory board;
- compiling and managing contact databases;
- putting in place administrative and financial procedures for managing the day-to-day work of the project.

The person appointed will be computer literate and familiar with a range of office applications including design and Web publishing packages. Programming skills and the ability to adapt existing educational technologies are desirable. A degree in the relevant subject area together with experience of supporting learning and teaching in this subject area are required, together with excellent interpersonal and communication skills. The person appointed will be a team player, able to self-motivate, use their initiative and display good judgement. She or he will be able and willing to carry out both highly skilled and mundane tasks with equal attention to detail.

Figure 5.1   *Jack or Jill of all trades*

Project staff therefore need to have the confidence and common sense required to plan and take forward areas of activity with the least drain on time and resources.

One size does not fit all

When considering the staffing needs of the project you should bear in mind that potential recruits are unlikely to fit the traditional profiles of staff grades adopted by universities. At the University of Warwick for example, members of staff are appointed to one of the following grades:

● academic/academic related;

● research;

● administrative/library/computing/(ALC);

● secretarial/clerical or technical grades.

Referring back to Figure 5.1, it is fair to say that the person required to fit this job description would span all these categories. This can create difficulties when drafting job specifications and deciding on the appropriate salary for project staff. It even impacts on the job title – for example, you may not be permitted to use the term 'administrative' (eg administrative assistant) for posts that are not on the ALC grade. In general, post titles within grades should equate to those in common use in the university.

While the university's recruitment procedure may allow for parity in the sense that staff on similar pay and grades may expect similar conditions of work, for projects such as the NCLE the necessity to fit the job description to a predetermined profile may potentially limit the field of suitable candidates. The representation of posts according to university grades and the connotations that these carry, particularly for applicants who are familiar with the university environment and working practices, may mislead potential applicants about the requirements of the post. Alternatively, potential applicants may be dissuaded from applying because they think they are not suitably qualified according to the usual criteria for university posts.

It is therefore important to ensure that the further particulars for the post clearly describe the nature of the job and the type of person that is required. Any further details that you can provide via the project's Web pages (where available) would be of assistance to potential applicants. It is also a good idea to circulate the details of the post to any contacts you have who might be interested, or who might know someone suitable. The services of organizations such as the National Coordination Team may also be called upon in disseminating the details of the post more widely.

MAKING PLANS

With funding of perhaps only three years and starting a project from scratch you can expect to spend the first nine months, maybe more, appointing staff, acclimatizing to the context in which the project operates and putting in place the organizational infrastructure. These early months are crucial and you should not feel that time is being wasted because there are no obvious 'deliverables'. As has been discussed, the staff are key to the success or otherwise of the project and it is essential to spend time defining job roles and person specifications. It is also important to ensure that when staff members are appointed they have the resources available to them to hit the ground running. Thus, work can begin more quickly if issues such as the allocation of office space, computer equipment, guidelines on office procedures and so on are dealt with in advance. Most important of all, the project manager needs to develop an operational plan that breaks down tasks, allocates resources and sets deadlines for completion. This will form the backbone of the project.

The operational plan

The operational plan, or project plan, is a document that sets out the key targets (usually on an annual basis) of the project, identifies activities to achieve the targets, and allocates resources and sets deadlines. Tasks in each year should relate to each other and combine to enable clear progression across all areas of activity. Not only does this provide a framework for ensuring that objectives can be met within the time frame and budget, but it also enables staff to see how their areas of responsibility feed into the work of the team as a whole. Thus, an operational plan will identify key areas of activity such as the development of a Web site, organization of events, production of newsletters and so on. You will need to ask yourself certain questions in relation to each activity, and record the answers on your plan.

Questions to ask yourself

- What are your targets for the year?
- How you will know you have reached your targets (in other words, what are your performance measures)?
- What steps will you need to take in order to reach your targets?
- When do you need to reach your targets?

- Who will take responsibility for reaching these targets and what support will that person need from other project staff?

- What are the financial implications of achieving these targets?

The operational plan should be reviewed on a regular basis and adjustments made as necessary. It is important to remember that however well laid your plans, they have a habit of being disrupted at times. Learning and teaching projects tend to be journeys of exploration: the operational plan is a rough map but it does not necessarily take account of road conditions and travelling companions! Neither does it alert you to sightseeing opportunities that arise along the way. Therefore do not be afraid of being responsive to new ideas and opportunities as they arise, and if they will add value overall to the work of the project, then you should consider adjusting your priorities. However, any final decisions on amending the operational plan in any significant way should be made only after consultation with your advisory board/steering group or other representatives from the subject community. Not only is it essential to have their support but it is also helpful to listen to the perspectives of those who are on the receiving end of the project's activities.

Example 1

An example of an unforeseen area of activity drawn from the NCLE is the establishment of the Learning in Law Initiative (LILI) network. The project team realized early on that to succeed at a national level the NCLE needed to establish key contacts in every law school. LILI grew into a network in its own right with an annual national conference. This had not been budgeted for, nor indeed had any resources been allocated to the support of a formal network. However, we realized that LILI was a useful mechanism for involving law teachers and giving them ownership of the work of the project. There was also a clear interest from the community in the establishment of such a network. Consequently plans were adjusted to accommodate this expanded area of activity.

On the other hand, despite the operational plan, you will from time to time hit dead ends or lose your way due to unforeseen circumstances. When this happens, try to salvage what you can from the experience and reflect on how the lessons learned can guide you in making future plans.

Example 2

Another example from the NCLE concerns the commissioning of publications on learning and teaching from law academics. We over-estimated the number of publications that we could successfully complete within three years (we planned for 12 and ended up with 6). It was incredibly difficult in several instances to hold the commissioned authors to deadlines, and a lot of time and energy was wasted on chasing for material. A related difficulty was the trouble that many of the authors had in writing about the pedagogy, as opposed to the various subjects within law. This required the project team to spend a significant amount of time working with the authors to emphasize the value of 'how to teach' as opposed to 'what to teach'. By the end of three years we were very proud of the six publications that were successfully completed. Another two were completed in draft form but did not meet the requirements of the agreement made with the authors. We therefore negotiated with them to provide 'summarized' versions of the copy provided, to be published on the Web site. This they were happy to do: the electronic medium seemed to make them more comfortable with providing what they perceived to be 'unacademic' commentary on their subject area.

All in all this experience of commissioning, editing and publishing a series of books provided a number of useful lessons in relation to planning activity:

- Be clear about the scope and purpose of the activity when it is allocated outside the project. Explore collaborators' understanding of what they are being asked to do – do not assume that the words you use will convey the meaning you intend!

- However well laid your plans, it is human beings who actually make them work. Be prepared for them to cause delays or at least diversions, and try to recognize when their way of doing things may in fact be better than, or at least as good as, yours.

- Be prepared to change your plans when it becomes clear that the level of resource being demanded to try and achieve them is becoming unsustainable and disruptive to other areas of activity.

MANAGING THE PROJECT

While the previous discussion has involved various aspects of project management, this section will consider in more detail questions relating to timetabling the project and managing the budget.

Keeping the project to timetable

The experience described in the previous section raises the question of how you can best keep the project to timetable, particularly when you are relying on non-staff members to provide all, or a significant part, of the 'deliverable'. Again, the operational plan will be your starting point within the project. All project staff should be allocated tasks and deadlines for completion, and regular staff meetings and informal discussions should enable the project manager to track progress and to pick up on any delays or difficulties. A project manager can maintain steady progress across all areas of activity by using the regular advisory board/steering group meetings or team meetings to focus staff on bringing areas of activity up to speed. The regular project newsletter will tend to have a similar effect since by its nature it requires fresh and interesting information about the work of the project. The project team should be expected to provide this input and also to use the newsletter as a vehicle for maintaining and generating interest in the project activity among the target community.

As far as keeping other, non-staff contributors to timetable is concerned, the project manager clearly has less direct control, as Example 2 tends to suggest. However, since a large part of the value, not to say the *raison d'être*, of learning and teaching projects is the involvement of the subject community, it is important that such outside involvement exists. There are a number of ways in which individuals or groups can be contracted to work with the project:

On a voluntary basis
This might manifest itself as a key contact within a department undertaking to distribute newsletters on behalf of the project. This works best where the person is an enthusiast about the aims of the project and keen to be involved. Where individuals are 'volunteered' (for example by the head of department) they are less likely to carry out their duties as punctiliously as you might wish. It is important to find ways of engaging with volunteers to ensure that they feel valued. Try the occasional e-mail consulting them about issues, providing them with forward notification of events or, as in the case of LILI, creating a formal network to give them a higher profile within the activities of the project.

On a fee basis

You could pay fees for the provision of written material or for the presentation of workshops. Where money is being offered, it is prudent to draw up a formal letter of agreement that sets out the expectations on both sides, including the schedule for delivery. Clearly, the use of documents such as these will not always guarantee compliance. However, the staging of payments according to the achievement of agreed targets is a useful way of both compelling activity and also limiting losses should activities not be delivered in full.

Buying out time

Where individuals or groups are working on specific projects for you, then you may want to consider 'buying out' a proportion of their time. This means negotiating with their head of department to free up part of their timetable (usually by reducing their teaching or administrative load) to enable them to undertake the work. The money is paid directly to the department, but the benefit to the individuals doing the project is that they get the support and time to concentrate on an area of interest to them. In theory this approach should be a good way of eliminating the excuse that other commitments have prevented completion of an agreed task. The head of department can also be asked to intervene if progress is not as rapid as expected. However, there is always the risk that a head of department will be happy to receive the money for the general departmental pot, but then fail to make appropriate provision to enable their staff to find the time to work on the project. The incentive for the members of staff concerned may also not be as great in this instance as it would be if the money were paid directly to them.

Secondment

This is where a member of staff from another institution spends a block of time working full-time for your project. This is a useful mechanism for securing specialist input on specific areas of activity. It is usual for the home institution to continue paying the salary of its staff member, but to invoice the project to cover the costs of this during the period of the secondment. The host (your project) is expected to provide an office for the secondee and other facilities necessary to enable him or her to do the work.

Keeping the project to budget

It is likely that as a newly appointed project manager you may not have much, if any, experience of managing what might be a large project budget. However, the process of putting together the operational plan will require you to make some estimate of the cost of each area of activity. In order to ascertain whether the scope of activity is affordable overall, you will need to work out how much of the activity is already paid for (because project staff will carry it out) and how much will need to be paid for separately. In order to do this it is suggested that you take a three-step approach, derived from the guidance provided to the LTSN subject centres by the LTSN Executive:

1. Separate any costs associated with fixed assets, such as staff salaries, overheads, office running costs, from the budget.

2. Separate out any activity that will be delivered by these fixed assets. For example, your Web site, administration of the events programme, and project management will probably all be delivered by the project staff.

3. The remaining amount is what is available to deliver all other activities specified in the operational plan.

This process should help you to fully appreciate and utilize the skills available among the project staff. It should also clarify how much money is available to achieve what you have planned. It is possible that the process will reveal that aspects of your operational plan are not affordable, in which case certain activities will have to be scaled down, or thought will have to be given as to how the aims and objectives can be achieved in other ways. You might consider approaching supporting organizations for matched funding, or seeking sponsorship for particular events from, for example, academic publishers.

However you end up profiling your budget, you should be able to draw confidence from the thorough preparation and costing of the operational plan. The advice about revisiting and revising the operational plan as necessary obviously applies to the allocation of funding, too. Expenditure should be monitored on a regular basis and the funding body will require that reports are made on the budget and expenditure, usually twice a year. Again, this is a useful incentive for keeping the budget in order, and for ensuring that the cost of activity represents value for money.

Working with the university's finance office

However, the best laid budgets are subject to any number of problems, and many of them are likely to centre on the relationship between your under-standing of the project's account and that of the university's finance office. Examples 3, 4 and 5 illustrate potential problem areas, and give comments and suggestions for addressing them.

Example 3

The university statement suggests that your account is in deficit by several thousand pounds despite the fact that your own accounts show that your funds are underspent.

Comment

In the case of the NCLE it transpired that the project funds had been paid into a general university profit centre and not allocated specifically to the NCLE project. It took several weeks before all project funds were eventually paid into a dedicated NCLE account, and a lot of correspondence about how much funding we should have received and at what times.

Suggestions

Make sure that the finance office receives a copy of the letter confirming your annual grant. Check that you can see the grant being paid into your account on a monthly basis, and be prepared to be persistent in getting any discrepancies addressed.

Example 4

The university statement shows items of expenditure that are a complete mystery to you.

Comment

Before the introduction of the SAP system (a computerized accounting system) at the University of Warwick, account holders were provided with monthly printouts of their income and expenditure. I used to go through each item and tick it off against my own records. Fairly regularly there would be a payment out that I did not recognize or, more occasionally, a payment in. This was usually because our code had been mistaken for that of another department. This still happens even now that the accounts are computerized.

Suggestions

Whatever accounting system is used, it is important to regularly marry up your records against those held by the university. Mistakes do happen, and you are more likely to pick them up if you maintain familiarity with the expenditure profile of the project.

Example 5

The university statement shows that identifiable items of expenditure are far in excess of what you expected to be charged (for example, for postage).

Comment

It is easy to overlook excessive expenditure on items such as postage and photocopying which tend to be charged by the university directly to your account, meaning that you do not have the opportunity to query them in advance.

Suggestions

Keep a record of large mailings. The NCLE had a set of scales to weigh non-standard items of post and each day the volume of mail going out was recorded to give us a view of monthly postage costs. Similarly, keep track of large volumes of photocopying and estimate your costs each month.

Reprofiling the budget and viring funds

Other difficulties that you might encounter relate to reprofiling the budget to take account of changes in priorities for the project. For example, you might find that you need to appoint extra staff, or that staff that you had budgeted for are not appointed and you therefore decide to use the underspend for a different purpose. In such cases, it is important to consult and to gain the approval of both your advisory board and the funding body. Similarly, if you find that you have not allocated enough money to a particular budget head and it is in danger of becoming overspent, you will need to consider viring money from elsewhere in the budget. Alternatively, you may be able to charge expenditure to other budget heads, thus avoiding the need to vire money from one to the other.

For example, if your postage budget is looking rather low, investigate where the money is going. Is it just on general correspondence or is it on items such as mailing out the newsletter? If it is the latter, then consider charging all postage relating to the newsletter to your publicity or dissemination budget. This is quite legitimate and does not require any consultation outside the project team, although you should, of course, keep complete records of what has been charged to which budget head and you must be able to explain why.

Remember that where it does become necessary to vire money from one budget head to another, you must seek the permission of the funding body in advance. It would not normally be acceptable to vire money from project activities into the staff budget.

FINALLY

Successful project management is a mixture of careful planning and opportunism. The firm foundation provided by thorough organization and a good project team should enable the project to evolve and grow. The examples and reflections offered here will, I hope, offer you an insight into how this may be achieved. Issues of resource management may appear rather uninteresting and secondary to the bigger mission of improving and enhancing learning and teaching practice. What you need to remember is that the better your project is managed, the more likely you are to meet your project's targets, and exceed them.

EDITORS' COMMENTARY

Organizational and financial skills are often not the most attractive part of the job description for the manager of an educational development project. Even other members of the project team – who usually benefit from the availability of good organizational and financial skills – may find the persistent attention of a good project manager to these issues wearing. One possible approach may be to focus on stakeholder contracts, using these contracts to clarify expectations all round.

It is at times of difficulty in a project that strong organizational and financial skills really prove very important. One such difficulty is when a member of a consortium project finds itself unable to continue the collaboration. At these times the existence of a consortium agreement can make a very difficult situation manageable. The use of a consortium agreement can make it possible to track work done against work expected, to apportion resources for work partly completed, and to redraw work plans among the remaining consortium partners. In one example of such a situation encountered by the National Co-ordination Team, the redrafting of a consortium agreement after the departure of a consortium member helped the two remaining partners to work much more closely together.

Project AMATAS, an FDTL Phase Three project based at the University of Central Lancashire, experienced a variation of this. Drafting consortium agreements often clarifies the work to be completed in such clear and explicit terms that project members can become alarmed at what is expected of them. This happened with Project AMATAS. When the consortium agreement was drawn up, it became clear that one party had no intention of doing the work within the appropriate time frame. However, someone else from the same department stepped in and became a very enthusiastic and positive contributor to the project. Six months later, that consortium partner had in fact delivered as per the agreement.

When the manager of another project left after about nine months, it became clear how far behind its milestones the project was. The project manager had been quite happy to let things slip and was not aware of the consequences of this action. At the interview for the replacement project manager, the directors were faced with two very competent candidates who had quite different backgrounds and skills. This made them re-evaluate the person specification for the job of project manager. This project is located in an Academic Development Unit where there are a number of experienced project managers already working. One of these other project managers had been covering the vacancy since the original project manager left. It was decided that subject-specific skills and knowledge were the essential elements for the successful management of this project, and that the management skills could be acquired more slowly by learning from those already in post. The new project manager has the required academic skills and credibility in the field, and is learning project management skills under excellent tutelage. She has been able to bring the project back on track by engaging with her community on the academic level, while having the back-up of an experienced project manager to teach her the skills she needs.

6

Riding out turbulence

June Balshaw and Howard Senter

INTRODUCTION

The TALESSI project (Teaching And Learning at the Environment–
Science–Society Interface) (FDTL Phase One) set out to enhance three interrelated aspects of students' environmental learning at the environment–
science–society interface:

- **interdisciplinarity** – the capacity to integrate knowledge derived from
  disciplines that may have very different views of what counts as valid
  knowledge;

- **values awareness** – appreciation of the insights afforded by environmental philosophy and ethics, along with the ability to recognize values
  that enter environmental debate via the supposedly 'value-free' natural
  and social sciences;

- **critical thinking** – in aggregate, the means to question and reveal the
  contestable character of 'knowledge claims' advanced in relation to
  many environmental questions, and to incorporate this critical
  awareness into students' own academic writing.

These aims reflect the changing character and balance of power within
environmental education. Once dominated by the 'hard' sciences, such as
Geography (in our context) and Earth Science, with their traditionally positivist paradigm, environmental education has increasingly shifted towards
being a 'crossroads of the disciplines' where Philosophy, Politics,
International Relations and Sociology are all making their voices heard.

A NEW PARADIGM

TALESSI's approach to learning and teaching sought to problematize the knowledge claims made from within the various disciplinary perspectives, in such a way as to reveal their epistemological bases and the way that values have entered into the environmental debate. This approach, which is anchored principally in the philosophy and sociology of knowledge, appears particularly helpful in making sense of the contested character of many current environmental issues – those where knowledge is uncertain and provisional in nature, and where conflicting views are heard, both within the groves of academe and beyond. These 'contested' issues include ozone depletion and global warming, the controversy surrounding organophosphates and oestrogenic chemicals, and of course matters such as pollution and the genetic modification of crops.

TALESSI's founders believed that it was necessary to challenge the prevailing epistemology of environmental higher education, a supposedly 'common sense' view of science which was typified by Chalmers as follows:

> Scientific knowledge is proven knowledge. [According to this view,] scientific theories are derived in some rigorous way from the facts of experience acquired by observation and experiment. Science is based on what we can see, hear, touch etc. Personal opinion, or preferences or speculative imaginings have no place in science. Science is objective.
>
> (Chalmers, 1988)

When taught according to this view, students are given to understand that any uncertainties and unresolved issues in the subject will eventually be replaced by certainty, as more resources are brought to bear and new knowledge, better equipment and better methods of analysis are adduced. This 'renders students blind to the subjective component that is present to some extent in all knowledge claims' (Jones, Merritt and Palmer, 1999).

The project team therefore sought to develop forms of critical thinking that would assist students in evaluating knowledge claims emanating from all the disciplines represented in environmental higher education, as well as those that are made in the broader public arena. The experience of the project was that this approach was valid – and that its validity could extend well beyond our target subject areas. The attempt to integrate the understandings of such different disciplinary approaches – although characteristically appropriate to our times – also represented a considerable challenge: indeed, more of a challenge than was at first realized.

As the abstract of a keynote article in the *Journal of Geography in Higher Education* put it:

> A key learning outcome of most, if not all, higher education is that students should be able to think critically about the subjects they have studied. This applies as much to broad-based undergraduate programmes in environmental higher education as elsewhere. In environmental higher education, this means that students should be able to think critically both within and across the various disciplines that constitute their study programme. An implication of this is that students need to have an awareness of the epistemological and value-based commitments that are present – though frequently unacknowledged – in all 'knowledge claims'; and in particular, that they should be sensitive to the ways in which these commitments often vary within and between different disciplines. Put another way, it is our view that awareness of epistemological and value-related questions is a prerequisite for critical thinking in environmental higher education. Moreover, in so far as critical thinking across disciplines enables students to integrate knowledges produced within different disciplines, these two kinds of awareness are also prerequisites for interdisciplinarity.
>
> (Jones *et al*, 1999)

THE CHALLENGES

The first – explicit – challenge was to develop a structure and a programme that could fulfil the project deliverables and outcomes. As a consequence of interviews and focus groups with practitioners and students, the outcomes identified for the TALESSI project were:

- a conference for environmental educators and others interested in promoting interdisciplinarity, values awareness and critical thinking;
- a series of staff development workshops;
- a project Web site;
- development and pilot testing of teaching and learning resources (TLRs);
- an archive of course materials.

In all of this, the project eventually succeeded – indeed some targets were exceeded – though it was necessary to reduce the number of practitioner interviews in the earlier stages of the project.

Second came the politico-academic challenge of overcoming resistance (which was often registered as 'lack of interest') from the 'hard science' end of the environmental education community, both within the host institution (the University of Greenwich) and more widely. This problem, although it was implicit in TALESSI's original aims and rationale, turned out to be more difficult to deal with than anyone had imagined.

Finally, there was a challenge that no one had predicted, and which had a significant adverse effect on the response to the inherent challenges of the project. This was the disruption caused by the reorganization of the departments involved in environmental education at the University of Greenwich. The project was 'orphaned', lost its way, and finally found a loving foster-parent.

THE ACHIEVEMENT

The project's specific deliverables included:

- a Web site, which was established in late 1997 and regularly updated thereafter;

- a two-day residential conference, which was held in April 1998 and was considered a success by the 40 participants;

- an initial target of 45 new teaching and learning resources, which was met, with 46 TLRs completed and a further two in usable draft form when the project ended;

- an archive of course materials, established in late 1997, which contains information from 80 departments in 50 different institutions, and is also regularly updated.

There was broad consultation with the teaching and student communities, and the need for a flexible approach rapidly became apparent. The original plan was to hold 30 interviews with practitioners, and five focus groups, as vehicles for disseminating and obtaining feedback on project plans and development. However, it was soon discovered that the interviews were less effective than the focus groups. Following discussions with Carole Baume at the NCT the balance was changed, and with 15 interviews completed, this aspect of consultation was scaled back and the number of focus groups was increased to 12. Five student focus groups were also held.

Workshops were another important vehicle for dissemination and feedback, with the main focus on peer review of TLRs. Again the original plan was modified in the light of circumstances, especially because regional workshops proved difficult to organize. Twelve workshops were eventually held, against an original target of seven, and more of these were held at the University of Greenwich than originally intended. Ranging in length from one hour to a full day, the workshops were also held at seven other institutions, with around 110 people participating. The aims of the workshops were to:

- promote dialogue, informal exchange and mutual understanding between project team members and the user community;

- raise awareness of the project and the issues it seeks to address;

- broaden and consolidate the participation of end-users in project activities;

- provide a forum for the discussion and dissemination of good practice;

- gain feedback on draft TLRs and proposed future activities.

A quality survey of workshop participants showed 84 per cent of respondents rating the workshops either 4 or 5 on a 1 to 5 scale (5 being high).

The other principal activity involving practitioners was the piloting of TLRs, which were the project's principal deliverable. A total of 81 piloting events (the target was 80) involved 21 institutions, and 33 individual users, with a further 20 institutions expressing interest.

This high level of participation undoubtedly helped the project team achieve very high quality in the TLRs, which proved to be considerably more substantial and educationally rich than had been anticipated. Although some participants commented adversely on the lack of practical advice, the TLRs have been commended for developing a critical and philosophically informed approach, for transcending disciplinary boundaries, and for supporting active and resource-based learning. When workshop and conference participants were asked to predict how widely the TLRs would be used, the response was:

- by self: 81 per cent;

- by others in my institution: 49 per cent;

- by others across environmental higher education more generally: 67 per cent.

The relatively low figure for 'others in my institution' may be a reflection of the sharply divided opinions about TALESSI's approach. The support and the take-up of the TLRs and other resources probably came mainly from practitioners who already agreed with the project's approach.

THE COURSE OF EVENTS

The original successful bid for the TALESSI FDTL project was made by the University of Greenwich's Department of Earth and Environmental Sciences in 1996. The project was due to start in October 1996. Almost immediately, one of the three prime movers of the project left for an extended secondment overseas. Shortly after this, the Earth and Environmental Sciences department was split up. Part of it moved to a site at Chatham in Kent, and other parts to various other locations, leaving the TALESSI project team behind in Greenwich, where it was eventually 'adopted' by the Department of Humanities. During this period, the severity of opposition, both from 'hard science' elements within the university and from the environmental sciences more widely, became fully apparent. This opposition centred upon the project's epistemological stance. The proponents of the 'scientific knowledge is proven knowledge ... science is objective' stance may then have felt some satisfaction on seeing a 'science' project that they considered spurious being folded into a 'humanities' bosom.

Who were these opponents of the project? Individual names are of course not the issue: opposition (or at any rate scepticism) lay deep in some parts of the teaching community. The TALESSI final report describes a spectrum of views:

- those who are sympathetic toward interdisciplinarity, critical thinking and values awareness of the kind advocated by TALESSI;

- those who display multidisciplinarity – with or without some inter-disciplinarity – but with little existing evidence of, or inclination to adopt, a 'critical' or 'value-aware' approach;

- those whose provision is mainly confined to the natural and physical sciences. Other disciplines are either absent, or play a subsidiary role in the curriculum; where present, they are often taught from a perspective (1) which does not favour critical thinking and values awareness, and (2) obscures the problematic nature of interdisciplinary integration.

(TALESSI Project Team, 2000)

While this characterization does not offer any breakdown of numbers, it is clear that TALESSI's natural 'supporters' represented a minority in the field, and were an even smaller minority in the 'hard science' sectors.

With ambitious goals, but beset by this combination of external and internal factors – and perhaps even shocked by the scale of opposition – the project initially floundered, and little progress was made in the first six months. Following the first reporting stage, in early summer of 1997, those with responsibility for overseeing FDTL became concerned about the project, and later that summer the university was warned that funding would be withdrawn unless certain conditions were met. One of these was that 'an experienced project manager should be appointed'. This was done in October 1997, when June Balshaw joined the project.

After her appointment, the project's momentum was restored, and an energetic programme of consultation, development and dissemination enabled TALESSI to catch up with its target dates. June stayed with TALESSI until October 1999, when she left to become Head of Combined Studies at Greenwich. June takes up the story here:

JUNE'S STORY

When I arrived, June recalls, I was both excited and relieved. Excited at the prospect of a new challenge and relieved to have secure employment for three years! However, the reality of my new position soon hit home.

I was aware that as a result of restructuring, the department that had successfully bid for FDTL funding Earth and Environmental Sciences no longer existed in its own right and that the School of Humanities (very much my territory) had offered the project a new home. What I did not know until shortly after I had accepted the post was that the university had almost lost the funding and that the appointment of a suitably qualified project manager was a condition of funding being continued. This, inevitably, gave me cause for concern and prompted several immediate questions. Would the NCT be forever looking over my shoulder and would this impact on what the project was aiming to achieve? Would process and procedure overshadow the academic elements of the project, with 'outcomes' so strongly emphasized?

Given that the network of people who supported TALESSI's aims was small – even dwindling, perhaps – and that the institutional base was more than a little insecure, it seemed to me that the first need was to get the programme of activities back on track. We needed to reconstruct our operational, political and academic base, and to achieve this it was essential (a) to demonstrate that we were capable of making progress with the project deliverables, and (b) to build up our network of collaborators. This implied, for the time being, at any rate, not worrying too much about the epistemological debates and, instead, ensuring that useful things were happening on the ground. One of the first tasks I set myself, therefore, was to produce an activity plan, which would show at a glance what the project was doing at any given time. This went in parallel with a push to ensure that key deliverables, which would enhance our network (especially the conference and workshops), were organized properly.

There were other problems that needed dealing with: for example the project budget. The slow start had led to under-runs, and it was soon evident that budget allocations were also at odds with the present needs of the project. With some trepidation I approached the university's Finance Department – on another remote site, the other side of London – and also the HEFCE officer responsible for FDTL in order to try to arrange some modifications. It was a pleasant surprise to be met with understanding and support in both cases. There proved to be no difficulty in reaching suitable arrangements, once the necessary approaches had been made.

With my background in marketing and management – coming late to the academic world, I had worked for Dun & Bradstreet and in the advertising industry – I was personally committed to making things happen. I was also experienced both in project management and in developing formal and informal networks of people. Thus, although I was only employed for two days per week on the project, I was able to mobilize resources that would develop the necessary practical focus, and give attention to administrative detail.

The early steps were practical ones. We got the Web site up and running, and created both a database of contacts and a customized Access database. I felt that although the project was strong at the top, in a sense we had too many 'managers' engaged in theoretical aspects of the project, and not enough 'workers' doing the day-to-day work. We tried to remedy this by developing effective but low-cost resources. For example, a final year student – Manuel – created the Web site, and continued to maintain it even after he left London and returned to Spain. (Of course, other arrangements had to be made in the longer run.) Another student created the database, and we employed a lab technician who was studying for an MA to maintain it. The balance of the project shifted further in 1999, when the Assistant Director of the TALESSI project took voluntary redundancy (though fortunately he continued to assist on a consultancy basis).

The measures taken from October 1997 onwards helped restore credibility and momentum to the project. Our most important initiative, however, was probably the two-day residential conference which took place at Greenwich in April 1998. Forty people took part, including four members of the project team and a few representatives from other FDTL projects. The most important outcome of the conference was that we managed to use it to establish a network of enthusiasts who proved invaluable in two ways: first, in helping us step up the dissemination work that, until then, had been languishing; and second, in providing a much stronger basis for running our series of workshops. These conference attendees were also instrumental in stepping up the vital work of trialling our main deliverable, the Teaching and Learning Resources (TLRs).

The TLRs

TALESSI was committed to creating 45 TLRs, but initially the team under-estimated the amount of time and effort needed to write – and then trial – these centrally important materials. At my suggestion, and using the new contacts that the conference and our dissemination activities were producing, we succeeded in widening the net of participants considerably. We also began to offer cash rewards for writing and piloting the TLRs. For example, we paid £100 for each evaluation report on a TLR. This helps to explain the high number of external piloting events that took place (81) and of expressions of interest in piloting (61).

The TLRs have generally been considered a great success, though of course the difficulty of ensuring their penetration into the 'hard science' end of our audience did not go away. A good example of the approach and themes of our TLRs is TLR22, 'The Cold Fusion Story'. This resource, which consists of tutor notes, a briefing sheet and a case study, is designed for class-based activities led by the tutor. It falls into the categories of 'contested science' and 'case studies', and is based partly on a book about scientific deception by Grayson (1995). As readers will be aware, cold fusion would have represented a scientific, economic and environmental breakthrough of the first magnitude: 'energy too cheap to meter'. In the event, its much publicized 'discovery', announced in 1989, turned out to rest on unreplicable experiments and a great deal of wishful thinking, if not actual fraud. Cold fusion is a story of scientific rivalry (two universities in Utah were working independently on the idea), career ambition, competition for funding, divisions between disciplines (most physicists rejected cold fusion in principle, while chemists tended to be more sympathetic to the idea), and accusations of inadequate scientific method.

Thus the learning outcomes for the 'Cold Fusion' TLR were that students should:

● have at least an elementary knowledge of cold fusion;

- be aware that a range of stakeholders were involved in the unfolding of the cold fusion story, and have some understanding of the ways in which their interests might have influenced the development and outcome of the story;

- have considered cold fusion as one of a series of scientific controversies in the environmental field, and explored the implications of such cases in relation to the nature of scientific investigation.

(See www.gre.ac.uk/ bj61/talessi/tlr22.html.)

This TLR also demonstrates clearly the nature of the challenge that TALESSI was posing to 'common sense views of science', where, as Grayson (1995) puts it:

> in the conventional view, scientific investigation is seen as the rational pursuit of objective truth which can be uncovered or explained through the development or testing of hypotheses using proven experimental techniques. Scientists are assumed to hold a set of moral values including an over-riding commitment to truth in the face of pressures which might be exerted by financial inducements, the desire for professional advancement and other factors.

CONCLUSIONS

Although TALESSI's project aims were widely seen as pertinent and useful, the depth and persistence of opposition to its approach and viewpoint came as an unpleasant surprise to the project team. The project was designed to develop an educational approach that was antipathetic towards much traditional thinking and towards many assumptions in the environmental sciences. It was particularly challenging for those who adhered to the positivist stance that is represented by the 'common sense view of science'.

There are several lessons that can be drawn from the TALESSI experience. The first is not to underestimate the scale of the challenges being faced. Wherever the aim is to introduce new ideas and new practices, scepticism, lack of interest and even outright hostility can be expected. It is essential to devise a realistic project plan in the light of these factors. In principle, this can be seen as a 'change management' task: the absolute centrality of establishing a solid network of collaborators and supporters who can help drive the changes through should be obvious.

In a project with big ambitions and a substantial budget, project management skills are needed. Many academics' expertise lies in other directions, and with so many individuals attached to projects on a fractional basis, it is difficult for them to acquire skills in managing educational development projects. In TALESSI's case, and no doubt in many others, we can see in retrospect that if a project manager/administrator had been in post from the outset, many of our difficulties would have been avoided, or at least greatly reduced.

It is also important to possess (and further develop) skills in the effective use of both modern communications and information technologies. The use of the Web site and databases was crucial to the project's eventual success. General communication skills of the traditional type are equally important.

Finally, we would emphasize the need to be flexible in the face of changing circumstances. TALESSI seems to have been subject to an inordinately large number of 'slings and arrows', but contingency is an issue for every project – all the more so when key staff are employed, as mentioned above, on a fractional basis. Once we learned to be quick on our feet, following up opportunities even when they were not part of the formal plan, and taking advantage of temporary resources such as keen students with IT skills, our fortunes revived noticeably.

And, of course, we should always remember that we are not alone. Despite the initial difficulties and disputes, there were many people who put themselves out to help us, in our own university, in our partner institutions, and of course in the FDTL National Co-ordinating Team. Help is there if you need it!

REFERENCES

Chalmers, A (1988) *What is This Thing Called Science?* 2nd edn, Open University Press, Milton Keynes

Grayson, L (1995) *Scientific Deception: An overview and guide to the literature of misconduct and fraud in scientific research*, British Library, London

Jones, P C, Merritt, J Q and Palmer, C (1999) Critical thinking and interdisciplinarity in environmental higher education: the case for epistemological and values awareness, *Journal of Geography in Higher Education*, **23** (3), pp 349–57 (see also www.gre.ac.uk/ bj61/talessi/paper1.htm)

TALESSI Project Team (2000) *The TALESSI Project: Final report*, University of Greenwich, London

EDITORS' COMMENTARY

The TALESSI project was fortunate in gaining an experienced project manager; other projects find themselves in the less fortunate position of losing one. And losing one towards the end of a project is particularly difficult. However, given the need for a project manager nearing the end of a contract to find further work, it should not be a surprise when it happens. The difficulty is exacerbated if the project partners are not in close communication with each other. (Perhaps surprisingly, a project manager with really good communication skills can reduce the amount of communication between the project partners.)

One new project encountered this situation when the project only had six months to run. The new project manager realized that communication channels had to be generated very quickly among project partners if the project was to conclude successfully. He set up very formal reporting and monitoring procedures using a synchronous communications tool (that is, software that allows real-time communication between project team members on different sites, while providing simultaneous shared access to information and on-line activities) on the Web. He also engaged his National Co-ordinator in improving communication within the project.

Worse than a project manager leaving, you might think, would be the departure of most or all of the core project team, including the author of the project proposal. In fact, for one IT-based project, this mass exodus brought good results. New project team members found it easier to engage a wide range of interest in the project from other universities, partly because they were able to allow different interpretations of the originally tightly held project model. These different interpretations enabled the output of the project to be adapted and adopted more widely.

The 'Skills plus' project, was set up in a standard way to have a project manager who would organize and collect the data himself. Unfortunately the person appointed received funding for a project that he could direct before he could start work for Skills plus. To deal with this the project director contracted out all the data collection to members of the project team and to others who would be in contact, for other purposes, with the potential respondents. For instance, the academics on the team, together with their own colleagues administered questionnaires to students in class (2,269 responses). Others, such as careers officers who were already going to talk to employers in the workplace, were contracted to ask a few more questions (a short, structured interview) for the purposes of this project. They were also able to interview graduate employees while they were in the workplace (97 graduates and 117 other associated workers). This revised structure involved the project director in slightly more work. However, the data were thus collected more cheaply than originally planned. The surplus funding was used to extend the data collection to unemployed graduates for triangulation of findings. An imaginative response to a failure to recruit thus brought unexpected benefits to the project!

7

Developing collaboration: finding ways through the treacle

Judith Thomas

INTRODUCTION

This chapter is based on my experience as part-time manager of the Self Assessment in Professional and Higher Education project (SAPHE). It covers various issues relating to developing collaboration including: getting started; reviewing the bid and clarifying the allocation of funding; monitoring progress; the external evaluator; managing more senior colleagues and using your authority as a project manager; whether the project counts as proper research; and bringing it all together.

The SAPHE project aimed to:

- develop, pilot and evaluate a variety of self- and peer-assessment tools;

- explore the relationship between self-assessment techniques and course content;

- develop staff and student skills of self-reflection and self-monitoring;

- disseminate information.

The project was instigated by the staff development unit together with the departments of law, social work and education at the 'lead site' university. The major disciplines involved were law and social work, with the education department providing pedagogic support.

To ensure the approaches developed were relevant across the higher education sector, each discipline built on existing links with neighbouring institutions. This meant that we had four different higher education institutions involved: an 'old university', a '60s campus' university, a 'new' (former polytechnic) university and a college of higher education. The people directly involved were drawn from nine different departments.

This rich mixture came together by a combination of intention, judgement and serendipity, creating challenges that were not necessarily apparent at the outset. The diversity gave the project great dynamism, and much of my time was spent ensuring that the inevitable tensions created by differing interests were productively resolved. This chapter analyses some of the problems encountered, explores how they were tackled, then offers tips based on my experiential learning.

GETTING STARTED

Problem

The first few months in post were probably the most challenging. The project had been running for five months by the time I started. The majority of the budget was firmly allocated and key staff, including the assistant project manager, were in post. There was an office base with a computer but a distinct lack of paper clips and envelopes. Metaphors about me needing to 'hit the ground running' were prevalent while I was reeling from the culture shock of starting in a new institution. My major concerns were how to work the photocopier, get a computer log-in and address the mysteries of room-booking systems. The new moon on a cloudy night was more visible than any induction programme and somehow, somewhere, the project bid that I had been sent prior to my appointment seemed to have disappeared into the ether or at least into the collective unconscious. All this was compounded by the fact that changes to the original budget meant that there was no administrative support and my role needed to be redefined in the light of staffing changes.

Given the time and energy people had expended preparing the bid, appointing staff and developing the project within their own setting, it was not surprising that I arrived to find a backlog of work and multiple expectations. People had been focusing on their immediate priorities, and they were highly relieved that the assistant project manager and I could move forward with organization, coordination and dissemination. Within three months of starting I had to achieve three major outcomes:

- The first annual report was due.

- I had to set up a steering group meeting 'as soon as possible'.

- I was urged to present the project at a departmental seminar 'sooner rather than later'!

Action taken

Part of my self-directed induction process was to visit each of the sites involved and meet with the key staff. This enabled me to begin forming relationships, identify what people had been doing and discuss their expectations of a project manager. It also helped me to appreciate something of the different contexts and some problems that needed attention. These issues were included on the first steering group agenda, which then informed the drafting of the annual report. The information gathered while consulting about the report produced material for the seminar and other dissemination activities. Morgan considers 'They [women] help to produce organizations that are "networked" where the *process* of doing things is as important as the end result or product.' (Morgan, 1998: 130, original emphasis). In my experience, paying attention to the process and using networks also has the advantage of achieving multiple outcomes.

Tip
Look for the connection between different activities. See them as part of a 'greater whole' rather than as discrete tasks.

REVIEWING THE BID AND CLARIFYING THE ALLOCATION OF FUNDING

Problem

The key people in each department had not necessarily been the ones consulted about the original bid and in some cases they had not even seen it. The bid was a crucial document as it outlined the expectations of each site and the allocation of the budget. Even where people have been involved in preparing a bid the majority of the detailed work is often done by just one or two people, so be prepared to remind people what has already been agreed. This is a common problem and not confined to academic circles! Fisher quotes the example of managers in Shell who gave their 'vision presentation more than 100 times': he then goes on to comment that 'remarkably there were still people who said they didn't know what the vision was!' (Fisher, 2000: 217).

Action taken

In the first few months the bid became my bible/guide/focus, and discussing it formed the basis of most meetings. As is often the case, protecting the time of staff allocated to the project was a major issue. Each of the six sites developing materials had been allocated funding for between half a day and a day a week to cover staff time. It was important to explore how the money was being used to give lead staff time to work on the project. In some cases this was relatively transparent, such as buying out time on a specific module so as to give a clear number of teaching relief hours that were tangibly identifiable. In others cases, funding was used in less visible ways: for example, putting together a number of different small grants to create an additional post covering admissions. This freed existing staff time for the project but was more difficult to quantify. In all cases it was important to identify, with managers and the nominated project staff, how funding was being used and ensure that it did not just disappear into departmental or university coffers.

Tips

Formal agreements at departmental or institutional level are necessary, but do break these down with the staff directly involved. Record what you have agreed in 'user friendly' language as a working agreement, or in notes of the session, then use these as a basis for regular review.

Trace the money and ensure that people understand how this is allocated.

MONITORING PROGRESS

Problem

Following on from 'Reviewing the bid and clarifying the allocation of funding', there was, not surprisingly, a high degree of anxiety about what 'they (HEFCE) were wanting' (at this stage we did not have any guidelines for reporting). I was struck by the level of concern and the way the question was constructed in terms of 'what do they want?', rather than 'what do we want to say?', or 'are we meeting our aims?'

Action taken

Having a detailed discussion and going through the bid section by section enabled us to identify progress and clarify the changes that had been made. In most cases we were clearly 'on target' with specific activities. Progress, limitations and changes were noted in a paper that was drafted for the steering group, so that changes could be formally ratified, and so that the strategies for tackling problems could be given the clear backing of the steering group. Space, time and attention were also given to finding out what was working and the project's progress towards major milestones. In a complex project with tight deadlines it is very easy to become driven by the next target, or to be problem-focused, thereby taking for granted what has been achieved. But if you acknowledge achievement, people are more likely to stay motivated and keep their energy high.

Tips

- Use project meetings to make progress very visible, acknowledge and validate achievement.

- Highlight problems so they are shared and get a mandate for action on issues that you have not been able to resolve.

- Negotiate, agree and formally record major changes with relevant people, for example HEFCE officers, consultants, steering group members, and so on.

EXTERNAL EVALUATOR

Problem

The people who had been central in the design of the evaluation strategy and who, it was anticipated, would lead this, had either retired or were on long-term sick leave. As a consequence of these unpredictable factors there was still no external evaluator a year into the project, despite various attempts to appoint one. Site staff were anxious about the lack of evaluation and were concerned that someone would come and ask for a different type of evidence or criticize practices after they had been implemented.

Action taken

Soon after starting I had to raise the problem with the head of school, who was also my line manager. A replacement from within the department started, but unfortunately severe health problems meant he too went on sick leave. In subsequent discussions we identified that staff within the department had heavy workloads and were already contributing to the project in a number of informal ways. We therefore decided that it would be better to contract out this service, and a colleague in a neighbouring university was approached, thus constructively resolving the situation. Using an evaluator from outside the lead institution was also helpful in that he was not managed by anyone involved in the project design or implementation.

Tips

Be prepared for staff changes and do not become over-reliant on lead staff or 'champions of the cause'; encourage them to develop their networks.

Some functions or services may be better 'bought in', rather than these tasks becoming additional burdens on departments that are already heavily involved. Buying in from the outside – where you have complete control over the resources – also reduces the conflicts of loyalties that may arise when you 'borrow' staff.

MANAGING MORE SENIOR COLLEAGUES AND USING YOUR AUTHORITY AS A PROJECT MANAGER

Problem

The situation outlined above was resolved, and I was fortunate in that the manager involved was totally committed to the project as well as to the need for independent evaluation. However, challenging people who are in a powerful position due to their position, expert knowledge, control of resources or the power of their personality is likely to affect all project managers, so it is worth further exploration. The way in which power operates in any organization is complex: as Gould suggests, 'Power cannot be reduced to any fixed point of reference ... but is fragmentary, inherently unstable and based on shifting alliances' (Gould, 1992: 13). In academia there is a system that purports to be collegiate while at the same time placing very high value on a strict hierarchy of academic qualifications. It is steeped in tradition and is overlaid by bureaucracy, and yet departments may still operate as systems of independent entities. Increasingly, projects involve more than one institution, thus compounding the complexity, with the added dimension of historical rivalries and the emerging pecking orders of league tables.

Action taken

The structure of various committees within the project design meant that it was possible for all interests to contribute to the decision-making process. The role that steering group meetings played in anticipating difficulties, trouble shooting and creating a safety valve was crucial, for example, in negotiating an agreement over intellectual property rights and developing an ethical framework for evaluation.

Through my regular telephone conversations, site visits or e-mail contact with sites, I would occasionally pick up rumblings of discontent. When these issues could not be resolved spontaneously, or when it was important to debate issues publicly, meetings were set up. Prior to the meeting, I would discuss the issue with the person concerned and we would look at the best way of resolving it at the meeting. This could involve them including the issue in their report, but sometimes it was best raised in a more neutral way, for example in my report or as a separate agenda item.

Project managers need to work collaboratively with the senior staff who chair key meetings. Prior to every steering group meeting, and in between if necessary, I briefed the chair on progress and potential difficulties. Together we looked at the action already being taken, what needed to be done, or whether it was safe to leave an issue to see if it was raised by others. The chair would then ensure that time and attention was given to all concerns, and emphasized the need to ensure that the minority agreed with the way forward and were not just persuaded or overruled by the majority. In these situations the chair of the steering group was explicit in his responsibility to the principle of collaboration, rather than primarily to the lead institution. Lukes (1974), in his analysis of hegemonic power, highlights that those whose real interests are being suppressed may not recognize this, so project managers need to recognize structural power differences, analyse them and work with others to create and maintain a climate that celebrates diversity.

Tips

- Be aware of how power operates: in some cases this will be obvious but it is more likely to be subtle.

- Ensure that minority concerns are identified and incorporated into the decision-making processes; allow for a 'bottom-up' influence as well as a 'top-down' one.

- Plan the agenda with the chair of the meeting and use your intuitive knowledge to explore how potential conflicts of interest can be resolved creatively. However, take comfort from Oakley's view that 'without conflict life is dead and art impossible' (Oakley, 1984: 80).

- Plan and structure meetings, negotiate the agenda, have a designated chair and ensure minutes are taken.

- Have different types of meetings or committees with different cultures in terms of the degree of formality. Use meetings to go beyond the 'public' aspects of the project and its targets, to explore the more nebulous areas.

- Where possible, rotate meeting venues, as this gives people a better idea of the different contexts, and is more equitable in relation to time and travel costs.

'IS THIS PROPER RESEARCH?'

Problem

Through various formal but mainly informal discussions it became apparent that there was some anxiety about the nature of the funding. Many colleagues were used to a more 'traditional' approach to research, where an idea is worked on and the outcome might be a set of recommendations that the researchers may or may not be responsible for implementing. The starting and finishing point of FDTL projects is different, as funding is allocated because departments have already developed expertise. At national meetings the imperative was to disseminate and convince others. However, potential converts needed more to go on than the fact that the Quality Assurance Agency had given an 'excellent' assessment or that we had been given funding to 'sell our wares'. As Ramsden says, 'academics are not given to flights of optimism; they are trained [towards] caution, criticism, doubt' (Ramsden, 1998: 139), so we were regularly challenged, and challenged ourselves, on the evidence base of our approach.

Action taken

The strategy used to tackle this challenge had two related dimensions. One was to use the assistant project manager's research background to provide staff with copies of relevant research papers. The other was to locate the project within a research paradigm (see Thomas, 1999). The evaluation strategy outlined in Table 7.1 shows the variety of methods used to review, evaluate and develop self-assessment.

Table 7.1 *SAPHE evaluation strategy*

Type	*Internal*	*External*
Site-specific	Staff review meetings Student evaluations	Project managers External evaluator
Discipline-specific	Regular (approximately 3 monthly) meetings with lead staff from 6 sites and project managers	External evaluator Conference presentations and workshops
Multi-disciplinary	Project steering group Joint subject review and planning meetings	Conference presentations and workshops

This strategy was implemented in a way that reflected the characteristics of action research that Elliot suggests pays 'direct attention to the importance of empirical data as basis for reflectively improving practices' (Elliot, 1991: 51). This approach also links with Meggison and Pedlar's model of staff development (Meggison and Pedlar, 1992: 8). Both these methods mirror self-assessment practices in that they follow a continual process of taking action, gaining experience, reflecting on the experience in order to learn and then creating new ideas and theories to inform future action. With these ideas in mind we used a structure (Figure 7.1), adapted from Kolb's (1984) learning cycle, as a conceptual framework to introduce self-assessment and to promote the concept of learning from experience.

Reason and Rowan's (1981) work on cooperative research also informed our thinking. This approach has been developed by researchers who see interaction between people as an essential element of a research process that is 'with and for' people rather than studying them as objective objects (Reason, 1988: 1). Cooperative research should include negotiating the involvement of the individuals, everyone contributing to creative thinking and aiming for authentic collaboration (Reason, 1988, 1994). The voices of students and their perceptions of self-assessment were integral to the process of developing materials and evaluating the project (see Dalrymple, 1999; James, 2000). In retrospect we could have involved students more at a structural level by having representatives on committees and the steering group. However, as Reason suggests, 'co-operative inquiry can range from

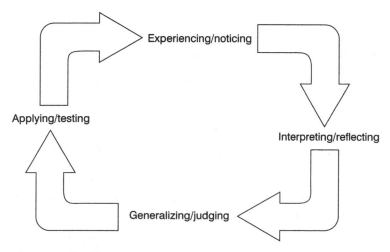

Figure 7.1   *Cycle of learning from experience*

full collaboration through all stages of the inquiry, to genuine dialogue and consultation at the moments of *project, encounter* and *making sense*' (Reason, 1988: 9, original emphasis).

In preparation for the six-monthly steering group, each site prepared a written report that was circulated prior to the meeting. These can be seen as the 'projecting' components, and helped people reflect while charting progress and problems. Early on in the project I had to resist suggestions that the project managers should write these as 'you know what we are doing' or that a verbal report would suffice, because differences in approaches would not have been so apparent, and the ownership of each site would have been reduced. Obviously a verbal report would have been time consuming and just available to those present.

Steering groups can feel like just a 'rubber stamp' or a ritual reporting but the 'encounters' were essential to the process of 'making sense'. By starting with reports from each site we were able to have a fairly open but rigorous discussion, not just on measurable targets and outcomes, but also on the subject of 'self-assessment'. The chair and those group members not involved with the daily running of the project explicitly played the 'devil's advocate' role, posing the sorts of questions cynics or sceptics might ask. This served us well, as the discussion promoted greater clarity, and also enabled us to rehearse arguments to the challenges we were meeting from colleagues or at conferences. It also created a culture of constructive challenge, while valuing the efforts of those involved.

Discipline-specific and interdisciplinary meetings were more informal than steering groups. These were the times when people could really offload problems, share tensions, celebrate success or, probably their most important function, tease out ways of creating change. Problems and differences could be re-framed as learning opportunities, and thereby inform self-assessment practices. Promoting what you are doing while you are still embedded in the messiness and uncertainty of it can be a strength if you do not gloss over the problems you are experiencing. One senior colleague identified that the credibility of the SAPHE project within his discipline was partly because 'we got our hands dirty developing it'.

Tips
Disseminate copies of papers that will support critical thinking in the area that you are developing.

Offer support and seminars to encourage teams to be research-minded in the way they develop materials. Do not accept the false dichotomy between research and teaching!

BRINGING IT ALL TOGETHER

Problem

The different types of educational settings involved in the project created challenges in that it was not easy directly to transfer methods and resources. Each site needed to develop self-assessment within its own context, culture and history, confirming Carr and Kemmis's view that:

> educational acts are social acts which are reflexive, historically located, and embedded in particular intellectual and social contexts. So knowledge about education must change according to historical circumstances, local context and different participants' under-standings of what is happening in the educational encounter. And it is clear that the knowledge we have will, to a very great extent, be rooted in local historical and social contexts.
>
> (Carr and Kemmis, 1986: 44)

To have tried to reduce diversity in order to get more easily comparable data or to construct a single reality would have risked undermining the impact of and the learning from undertaking self-assessment within these different contexts. (See Burgess *et al*, 1999, Hinett and Thomas, 1999, Hinett *et al*, 1999, for further discussion of the development of self-assessment within the different disciplines and sites.)

However, we did need to deliver on joint publications and conferences. Colleagues were keen to come together to learn from each other, debate and analyse the discourse of 'self-assessment', but transforming the direction given by the steering group or by discipline-specific meetings into concrete dissemination activities was more problematic. The timescale of the project and the time and effort of getting everyone together meant that such meetings had to move things forward in a tangible way. This was easier said than done, and there were a number of good reasons that moving into action was difficult. For example, some people were happy writing and disseminating for their own professional groups but were concerned about whether joint publications and multi-professional conferences would be relevant to our various audiences. There was also anxiety about the type of publication we could/should produce. Some people in the project had well-established publication records, while others were new to publishing, particularly in relation to teaching and learning.

Action taken

Taking time to explore such tensions and concerns in a safe way enabled us to find creative solutions. When preparing for meetings, as well as thinking about the content and clarifying the objectives of the meetings, I thought about the process and had structures in mind that I could introduce to draw out different views or that would help us look at things in a fresh way. At one meeting we undertook a SWOT analysis to identify the strengths, needs, opportunities and threats that people anticipated around the joint conference. An outcome of this was that, later on, we made sure that conference information clarified whether sessions were discipline specific or generic. Another concern, where two sites were critical about the way in which they had introduced self-assessment, was resolved by their offering a joint workshop based on the lessons they had learnt from their mistakes.

When we were struggling to move forward on a joint publication I used images of stars and potholes, to draw attention to the fact that we could get stuck in the potholes of difficulties or look to the stars and concentrate on the significant strengths and support we had (see Morgan, 1998, for more ideas on the use of metaphors and images, and Thomas, 2000, for how these techniques were used in the SAPHE project). This combination of free thinking and the firm but supportive backing of our FDTL consultants helped us decide on the format of a publication that would provide a coherent synthesis of the different authors, disciplines and institutions. We finished the meeting with a vision of the publication and a timescale for writing. Reaching an agreement on this subject led on to the next challenge – of ensuring it happened and not getting diverted by the many brilliant but totally different ideas people had by the next time we met!

Tips

- Recognize that group processes need to support the task, so allow time and space to explore the concerns of all involved.

- Look at how any risks can be minimized by being clear about target audiences, and communicating this rather than setting up false expectations

- Anticipate difficulties and identify strategies for moving on.

- Once you have collectively negotiated and agreed ways forward watch out for the mavericks who could innocently but effectively divert you.

CONCLUSIONS

While managing the project I was often aware of two key functions of my role. One was to be aware of and 'hold' anxiety rather than get caught up in a spiral. The other was to keep track of what was going on, and to try to understand why. Morgan suggests that managers 'must become skilled at "reading" organizations from different perspectives and at developing action strategies that are consistent with the insights they glean.' (Morgan, 1998: 4). All projects present a myriad of problems: the challenge for project managers is not to be daunted but to see these as opportunities for learning through the process of discovery and collective problem solving.

Each project will have a different set of complexities, personalities and problems, so your response needs to be founded on the strengths and resources available, and to use structures – such as different committees – to serve the project rather than just fulfil bureaucratic functions. I hope this chapter has given you some idea of the multitude of challenges to engage with. The tips will help you identify the things that merit further exploration and are offered as food for thought rather than a set menu – savour the flavour and enjoy!

REFERENCES

Burgess, H, Baldwin, M, Dalrymple, J and Thomas, J (1999) Developing self-assessment in social work education, *Social Work Education*, **18** (2), pp 133–46

Carr, W and Kemmis, S (1986) *Becoming Critical: Education, knowledge and action research* (1997 edn), Falmer Press, London

Dalrymple, J (1999) Student participation in evaluating self-assessment, in *Staff Guide to Self and Peer Assessment*, ed K Hinett K and J Thomas, OCLSD, Oxford

Elliot, J (1991) *Action Research for Educational Change*, Open University Press, Milton Keynes

Fisher, K (2000) *Leading Self-Directed Work Teams: A guide to developing new team leadership skills*, McGraw-Hill, New York

Gould, N (1992) Anti-racist social work: a framework for teaching and action, *Issues in Social Work Education*, 14, p 1

Hinett, K and Thomas, J (eds) (1999) *Staff Guide to Self and Peer Assessment*, OCLSD, Oxford

Hinett, K, Maughan, C, Lee, B and Stanton, K (1999) Managing change in assessment and learning in legal education: a tale of two cities, *The Law Teacher*, **33** (2), pp 135–58

James, D (2000) *External Evaluation Report: The SAPHE project* (unpublished paper), University of Bristol (available from SAPHE Web site)

Kolb, D (1984) *Experiential Learning*, Prentice-Hall, London

Lukes, S (1974) *Power: A radical view*, Macmillan, London

Meggison, D and Pedler, M (1992) *Self Development: A facilitator's guide*, McGraw-Hill, London

Morgan, G (1998) *Images of Organization: The executive edition*, Berett-Kohler & Sage, San Francisco

Oakley, A (1984) *Taking it Like a Woman*, Fontana, London

Ramsden, P (1998) *Learning to Lead in Higher Education*, Routledge, London

Reason, P (1988) *Human Inquiry in Action*, Sage, London

Reason, P (1994) *Participation in Human Inquiry*, Sage, London

Reason, P and Rowan, J (eds) (1981) *Human Inquiry*, Wiley, Bath

Thomas, J (1999) The challenges of developing self assessment practices in different disciplines and institutions: educational development or educational research? *European Journal of Open and Distance Learning* (EURODL) [Online] http://kurs.nks.no/eurodl/eurodlen/index.html

Thomas, J (2000) Collaboration in project management, *FDTL/TLTP Projects News Bulletin*, 5.

EDITORS' COMMENTARY

Getting the most from people associated with the project, whether or not they are formal members of the project team, is a task that challenges all project managers. A Teaching and Learning Technology Programme project 'Implementing Pharma-CAL-ology' took the approach of contracting members of staff from different universities to write teaching and learning resources. The project manager required each of these authors to set up a small advisory board to oversee the development of each resource. To maintain liaison across this development, the project manager became a member of each of the advisory boards. The authors and their advisory boards also met each other at the annual subject association conference. They reported that the opportunity to meet for a sustained period, and to use the social time between formal sessions for additional interaction, benefited the project greatly. In fact, the project managed to generate far more teaching and learning resources than had been originally planned.

Using the members of a steering group constructively is a topic considered by Angela Smallwood in Chapter 4. One FDTL Phase Three project, Better Together, seeks to gain double benefit from the members of its steering group by inviting them to an ideas-generating or materials-testing workshop immediately before the steering group meeting.

Another FDTL Phase Three project, the Performance Reflective Practice project (ReP), also engages a wider project membership in a creative way. This project, which focuses on reflective practice in dance, is using a travelling roadshow as its major dissemination method. The project manager is using the development of this roadshow as a method for exploring the wide range of approaches that different departments take to developing reflective practice with their students. Alongside the development of the roadshow, the project team is running a more formal programme of investigation into the theoretical basis of reflective practice. The project team reports that this parallel development method is allowing greater collegiality between departments and a clearer focus for the topic of reflective practice. The skill of the project manager is in ensuring that the two strands of development genuinely enrich each other. This demands considerable interpersonal skills as well as good planning.

Using project team meetings and steering group meetings as part of the system to monitor progress is also a good management tool, in that it uses existing structures and time already committed (that is, the meetings). The approach not only formalizes the information through the reporting process, but also makes all members aware of the project's progress against the plan. Many projects build the monitoring of the various project elements, such as finance or dissemination, into formal meetings by having them as standing agenda items.

This chapter also raises the difficulty caused by the different paradigm of research into practice. Judith Thomas poses the question 'is research into practice proper research?' For many academics who still adhere to the positivist paradigm as the only measure of 'truth', any phenomenological approach, that is an approach that sees reality as socially constructed rather than objectively determined, is bound to draw criticism. It is important that any research is based on an explicit and defensible paradigm and method-ology. Projects in education settings are inquiring into human processes such as learning and teaching. Many defensible qualitative methods can be employed. In many cases the positivist criticism of qualitative research is akin to saying that your boat is not a valid train! No: it's a boat. It's not meant to run on rails, it's meant to travel through water. Both boats and trains are valid methods of transport.

8

Making an impact through dissemination

Phil Gravestock

INTRODUCTION

The ultimate goal of any dissemination strategy must be the adoption of a project's outputs by the end-user. The common problem for all projects is how to do this effectively. In the same way that there has been a recognition that teaching is more effective if it is student-centred rather than subject-centred (see, for example, Biggs, 1999), there has also been a recognition that dissemination is more effective if it is centred on the end-user, with the content, media, style and language of the materials to be disseminated being carefully matched with the needs and requirements of the end-users (see Westbrook and Boethel, 1995; NCDDR, 2001).

Dissemination will be limited if it simply involves the sending of information to the target audience in the form of, for example, books, journal articles or CD-ROMs. Effective dissemination requires the end-user to be aware of the project as early as possible and to have a detailed knowledge of the nature and content of the outputs so that considered judgements can be made about whether or not to use the material (Fincher, 2000). Dissemination is therefore not a single act; it is a process involving several mechanisms throughout the life of a project, each aimed at a different dissemination goal. It is therefore important to ensure that careful consideration of a dissemination strategy occurs at the beginning of a project, not at the point when the final product is ready for distribution (NCDDR, 1996a, 2001; HEFCE, 1998). Previous information aimed at designing effective dissemination strategies (see Westbrook and Boethel, 1995; King, 2000; NCDDR, 2001) has highlighted the importance of the following elements:

- the source: its perceived competence and credibility;

- the content: its relevance for the users, and its cost effectiveness;

- the medium: its flexibility and accessibility;

- the user: their readiness to change and preferred dissemination media, and the level of contextual information needed.

This chapter concentrates on the dissemination strategy for the Dissemination of Good Teaching, Learning and Assessment Practices in Geography project, which was run by the Geography Discipline Network (GDN), and which formed part of Phase One of the Fund for the Development of Teaching and Learning (FDTL) initiative. As GDN Project Officer I was involved with the day-to-day running of the project, and with the implementation of the various dissemination mechanisms.

BACKGROUND AND CONTEXT OF THE PROJECT

In 1994–95 the geography provision in all higher education institutions throughout England and Northern Ireland was subjected to Quality Assessment by the Higher Education Funding Council for England (HEFCE). A Subject Overview Report was published (HEFCE, 1995) which noted several positive points about the provision of geography in England and Northern Ireland, but also noted several areas where there was room for improvement, summarized in Healey and Gravestock (1997) as:

- over-dependence on lectures (and hence the need for diversity and innovation);

- variable quality of tutorials and seminars;

- problems with laboratory, practical and fieldwork sessions;

- problems relating to undergraduate dissertation supervision;

- the need to strengthen links with employers and the world of work;

- assessment issues (for example, more feedback, bunching of marks);

- curriculum design issues (for example, progression between years 2 and 3; unequal treatment of joint honours students);

- the need to do more to share good practice.

The aim of the FDTL project was to identify and disseminate good teaching, learning and assessment practices in geography. To achieve this aim, one of the main outputs of the project was a series of 10 guides, aimed at geography staff in higher education (see Appendix), which would address the areas requiring improvement. The guides would be aimed at an international audience and would be based around a selection of case studies of effective teaching, learning and assessment practices in geography in higher education.

The project team consisted of a consortium of nine higher education institutions, representing a mixture of old and new universities and colleges of higher education. A geographer and an educational developer represented each consortium institution, although in some cases the educational developer acted as an advisor rather than a co-author. All members of the team were chosen for their expertise in teaching and learning in geography and/or educational development. An essential aspect of the dissemination of information is that the source has to be credible and that the end-user must be able to trust and rely on the information presented (King, 2000; NCDDR, 2001). It was therefore important to ensure that the team would be viewed as experts. Many of the geographers on the project team had worked on national initiatives such as the *Journal of Geography in Higher Education*, the Higher Education Study Group of the Royal Geographical Society with the Institute of British Geographers, and the Department for Education and Employment (DfEE)-funded discipline network.

DISSEMINATION

Purposes of dissemination

There are different levels and purposes of dissemination, and it is important to match the dissemination mechanism with the dissemination objective (Fincher, 2000). Three objectives of dissemination have been recognized (NCT, 1999; Fincher, 2000) which should be incorporated into any dissemination strategy:

- **Dissemination for awareness.** The target audience needs to be aware of your project, through effective publicity and marketing. *Know your intended end-user and make sure that they know you* (NCDDR, 1996b). Dissemination mechanisms may include conference displays, electronic messages to listservers, flyers and handouts, press releases and Web pages.

- **Dissemination for knowledge/understanding.** The end-users need to have a detailed knowledge of the outputs from a project in order to determine whether or not the material would be of use in their particular situation. It is important to ensure that this detailed knowledge is easy to obtain. Dissemination mechanisms may include newsletters, detailed handouts, workshops and Web pages.

- **Dissemination for use/action.** It must be the intention of every dissemination strategy to make sure that the outputs are adopted and used by the target audience, with the ultimate hope that some change will occur as a result of using the material.

Modes of dissemination

Fincher (2000) also distinguishes between two different modes of dissemination:

Active dissemination
This is where the intention is to provide information proactively about the project or outputs: for example, a press release coinciding with the launch of a product or a series of conference presentations.

Passive dissemination
The outcome of the dissemination may not be immediate: for example, placing material on a Web page so that it may be viewed by a potential user at any point in the future.

The project's dissemination strategy

Although the definitions of dissemination described above were not published when the project started, it is possible to show (see Figure 8.1) how the dissemination strategy adopted fits into these different categories.

Dissemination for awareness

One of the intentions of the project was to involve the end-users in as many stages of the project as possible, as dissemination is more effective when there is a two-way involvement between the source of the dissemination and the end-user (NCDDR, 2001). This was done by:

- **Creating a product for which there was a demand by the end-user.** This was particularly important for the UK target audience who wanted a product to address the issues raised by the Subject Overview Report,

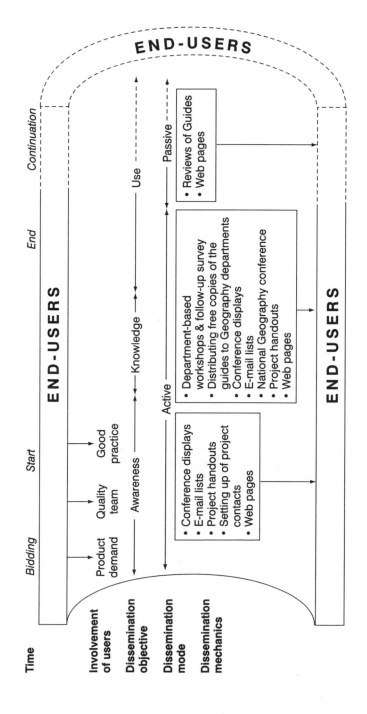

Figure 8.1 *Key elements of the project's dissemination strategy*

but it was also important to ensure that the outputs would be appropriate for a wider, international, audience.

- **Involving end-users in creating the project team.** The geographers in the team were taken from the group of end-users: that is, they were geography lecturers who were facing the same problems as the target audience, such as larger class sizes and diminishing resources.

- **Obtaining the case study examples of effective practice from the discipline.** It was important that the case studies were not solely generated by the team. The end-users needed to have an ownership of the project, and this was achieved by the users providing the raw material around which the guides were based.

The start of the project was a period of active dissemination, with mailings of project information to all geography departments in England and Northern Ireland. In order to ensure that these mailings would be reaching the most relevant person, departments were asked to provide a named contact person who had an interest in teaching and learning issues. Once the list of departmental contacts had been established, the project sent out a request for case study abstracts showing effective or innovative practice in the teaching, learning and assessment of geography in higher education.

It was apparent at the start of the project that if the guides were to be the sole repository of information there would be an initial phase of information gathering, followed by a hiatus during the middle phase of the project while the guides were being written, with a final phase of distribution and dissemination of materials at the end of the project. Such a model would have resulted in a piecemeal involvement of the end-user, with the potential of a loss of awareness of and interest in the project in the middle stage. It was therefore decided to use the Web to host the resource database of case study examples, which resulted in a fairly continuous stream of examples. These went up on to the Web quickly, and at the same time acted as resource material for the writing of the guides. It also meant that the project immediately had something to 'sell' through its promotional handouts, e-mail messages to listservers and conference displays, and that the progress of the project would be continuously on view to the end-user.

Dissemination for knowledge/understanding

Active dissemination mechanisms such as free distribution of the project's outputs, a national residential conference and department-based workshops were used to aid dissemination of knowledge to the end-user.

Personal interaction with the end-user is an important method of dissemination (NCDDR, 1996b), and the department-based workshops provided a particularly effective mechanism for the dissemination of knowledge. The authors of each guide provided a series of four or more workshop modules, which focused on different parts of the guide. Each module was broken down into a series of activities, with the intention that any member of the project team would be able to run any of the workshops for the guides. In order to help departments to choose which guides and workshops would be most appropriate, a précis of each guide and a summary of the workshop module contents were provided in a booklet and on the project's Web pages. The modular nature of the workshops also meant that they could easily be tailored to meet the specific needs of the department, after consultation with the named contact person.

The activities within the workshop modules ensured that departmental staff had to engage with the material within the guides, and think about how the case study examples could be used or adapted for their particular context. These workshops were particularly successful when combined with departmental 'away-days', where there was a 'captive' audience. When this was not possible, the project tried to arrange with the host institution to hold the workshop at a venue that was not within the relevant department, and was preferably off-campus, in order to encourage staff to remain for the whole event. This method of dissemination meant that the project could reach the 'agnostics' rather than continuously 'preaching to the converted', which can be the case with national or regional workshops where staff are invited to attend. The workshops also provided an excellent opportunity to find out about interesting practice in other departments and to encourage departmental staff to contribute abstracts to the resource database.

The final published versions of the guides were officially launched at a two-day national conference 'Improving teaching, learning and assessment in geography', held in September 1998, and attended by over 120 geographers and educational developers. A complimentary set of the 10 guides was sent to all geography departments in England and Northern Ireland, and a copy of the relevant guide was sent to all workshop participants.

Dissemination for use/action

It is recognized that this is a difficult area to evaluate, and in which to determine whether change has occurred (HEFCE, 1998; Fincher, 2000). Anecdotal evidence can be gathered to determine whether the case study material in the resource database and the guides themselves have been used and referred to (for example, hits on specific case study Web pages, telephone calls to the originators of the case studies for additional information, or conversations with colleagues at conferences), but it is difficult to determine whether actual change in practice has occurred in higher education geography departments.

Passive dissemination mechanisms

Several forms of passive dissemination were set up, so that information about the guides and the resource database would be available after the end of the project, such as information on the project's Web pages, and reviews of the guides in international journals.

PROBLEMS THAT WERE ENCOUNTERED

One of the main problems has been the assessment of the amount of change that has resulted directly from using the information in the guides and the resource database. The goal of any dissemination strategy is utilization (Westbrook and Boethel, 1995; Fincher, 2000; NCDDR, 2001), and the main aim of the project was to disseminate good practice, and thereby to create a change in practice so that the students would benefit from improved teaching, learning and assessment methods. The project conducted several telephone interviews with the departmental contacts about 3–6 months after a workshop had taken place, to try to determine whether any change had occurred as a result of attending the workshop and using the guides. From the responses obtained it appears that many departments had noticed a change in their teaching, learning and assessment practices at either an individual or a department level (see box), but this was change on the part of the lecturer, and not necessarily in the student experience. Determining the direct benefit for the students was beyond the scope of the original FDTL project, but is something that needs to be considered for future projects of this kind, possibly by concentrating on student feedback and external examiner reports.

Another problem encountered was the resistance of a few participants at the department-based workshops to some of the proposals and method-

---

Sample responses from the workshop follow-up survey

Are you aware of teaching practices, either departmentally or individually, having changed as a result of the workshop?

- We have designed a new MGeog course. Its format has been influenced by the workshop.

- We have a totally new set of guidelines for dissertations now.

- It has had an impact on how some individuals approach particular courses.

- Essentially it has made us think why we are doing assessment, what we are doing assessment for and whether it is appropriate.

Is teaching spoken about more? Is there more discussion within the department and a sharing of strategies and teaching methods?

- There has been a conscious follow through as a result of the workshop. ... We haven't let the ideas from the workshop die!

- Without a doubt. It has increased a great deal.

- We are now talking about ways in which we can introduce resource-based learning.

- The profile of teaching and assessment has been raised.

---

ologies in the case studies. King (2000) noted that this resistance might imply not that the participants were being stubborn, but that they did not believe there was a need for change. This highlights the fact that for effective dissemination to occur, a detailed knowledge is required of the context in which the end-user is working (Westbrook and Boethel, 1995; King, 2000), and in some cases it was important to know the internal influences that were facing a department, as these often offer a greater lever for change than external influences (NCDDR, 1996b). A telephone interview was conducted between the workshop facilitator and the departmental contact prior to the workshop to ensure that the material presented would be tailored to departmental needs. What was particularly important throughout all the department-based workshops and the guides was that the project explicitly avoided giving the impression that the current practice of the department or individual was wrong, ineffective or outdated in any way, as such an approach does not encourage either effective change taking place, or the embedding of such change (NCDDR, 1996a).

LESSONS LEARNT AND THEIR APPLICABILITY TO OTHER DISCIPLINES

Part of the success of the FDTL project must be attributed to the fact that geographers are responsive to new ideas, and that geography in the UK has had a 30-year history of developing discipline-based teaching and learning initiatives (Healey, 1998). In addition to the Geography Discipline Network, there were a number of other important learning and teaching initiatives in geography that were active at the time of the FDTL project: the *Journal of Geography in Higher Education*, which was founded by Alan Jenkins and David Pepper in 1977; the Higher Education Study Group of the Royal Geographical Society with the Institute of British Geographers, which was founded in 1980; and GeographyCal, which was a consortium team developing computer-aided learning packages for undergraduate courses in geography (Healey, 1998).

In any situation, it is worth considering the following suggestions, the implementation of which will increase the chances of successful dissemination, regardless of the project or discipline.

Suggestions for making dissemination successful

There has to be a **demand for the product** (NCDDR, 1996a; Fincher, 2000; King, 2000). An often-used analogy is that of marketing a new mousetrap. Just because it is new does not mean that people will rush to buy it. The target audience must: have mice; be bothered by the mice to the extent that they feel they need a mousetrap; feel comfortable with the effects of the mousetrap on them, their household, the mice and the broader environment; have the confidence to use the mousetrap; be able to afford the mousetrap; and believe that this mousetrap is an improvement on the one that they had already bought or were thinking of buying.

Make sure that your **target audience is aware of your project**, its aims and its outputs. Raising awareness of the project should be one of the first activities of the project, and should continue throughout the project to ensure that 100 per cent of the target audience knows about the project and what it is doing.

Make sure **mailings are reaching the appropriate person**. Many mass-mailings to educational institutions will target the head of department. In the vast majority of cases this will not be the most relevant person to read the material. It is essential to compile a database of relevant contacts who are interested in the material that is sent to them, and who will act upon the information presented.

Change has to come from the end-user (Fincher, 2000). In order for change to occur, the end-user must trust and rely upon the material being disseminated. One of the most important aspects of the GDN project was that the outputs were produced by geographers for geographers, in order to reduce the impact of the 'not invented here' syndrome. The fact that the team members were seen as both experts and peers meant that the end-users could trust the information within the guides.

In order to enhance change, the end-user needs to concentrate on **small discrete packages of information** (Fincher, 2000). The GDN project disseminated case study examples of effective practice, most of which were aimed at changing the practice of individual lecturers, for example by providing a different method of performing group assessment. Adoption of the ideas described in many of the case study abstracts would not have necessitated a substantial change to the lecturer's existing practice.

Concentrate on the end-user at all stages of the project. As Figure 8.1 illustrated, an awareness of the end-users needs to be present throughout the project. This model can be compared with a stick of British seaside rock – a traditional pink mint-flavoured candy stick which has the name of the seaside town from which it is bought running right through the centre – in that the end-user will be present at all stages of the project.

Make sure that there is a **match between the product and the user** (Westbrook and Boethel, 1995; NCDDR, 1996b; NCDDR, 2001). The final product needs to be matched to the end-user in terms of the content, media of presentation, format and language used. In the case of the GDN project it was always the intention to produce a series of guides that would be acceptable to an international audience. Therefore the language of the guides had to be appropriate, and it was important to ensure that there was not too much of a UK bias to the content. The project used international advisors from Australia and the United States to ensure that the language used in the guides was appropriate to a wider audience.

Think about **other potential audiences**. Although the guides were aimed primarily at international geographers in higher education, it was also the intention that other discipline specialists could use them, which is one of the reasons why experts in educational development were involved in writing the material. Although the guides contain geographical case studies, the educational principles were written in a generic manner. This has been an important reason for their success, with other disciplines such as engineering adapting the case studies for their own use.

Get the **support of national/international discipline bodies**. One other factor in the success of the project was the valuable support of discipline-based groups and bodies such as the Conference of Heads of Geography Departments in Higher Education Institutions, the Royal Geographical Society with the Institute of British Geographers and its associated Higher Education Study Group.

CONCLUSIONS

Dissemination is not a unitary activity or 'event', and effective dissemination strategies require several mechanisms addressing different levels and goals (Fincher, 2000). The Geography Discipline Network project used a number of active dissemination mechanisms such as conference papers and displays, e-mail messages to listservers, promotional handouts, a national conference and department-based workshops. The most successful of these activities, in terms of dissemination of awareness and knowledge, was the series of department-based workshops, which provided an opportunity for personal contact between the project team and the end-users.

Change can only take place by the actions of the end-users, and it is essential that they have ownership of a project. In this case the ownership was built not only through the fact that the project was discipline based, but also because the end-users were also contributors, supplying the core material – the case study abstracts – for the resource database and the guides.

REFERENCES

Biggs, J (1999) *Teaching for Quality Learning at University*, Society for Research into Higher Education (SRHE) and Open University Press, Buckingham

Fincher, S (2000) From transfer to transformation: towards a framework for successful dissemination of engineering education, paper presented at the 30th ASEE/IEEE Frontiers in Education Conference, 18–21 October 2000, Kansas City. [Online] http://fie.engrng.pitt.edu/fie2000/papers/1269.pdf (accessed May 2002)

Healey, M (1998) Developing and disseminating good educational practices: lessons from geography in higher education, paper presented to the International Consortium for Educational Development in Higher Education's Second International conference on Supporting Educational, Faculty and TA Development within Departments and Disciplines, Austin, Texas, 19–22 April 1998. [Online] http://www.glos.ac.uk/gdn/confpubl/iced.htm (accessed May 2002)

Healey, M and Gravestock, P (1997) *Identifying and Disseminating Good Practice in the Teaching and Learning of Geography in Higher Education* [Online] http://www.glos.ac.uk/gdn/confpubl/iagaag.htm (accessed May 2002)

Higher Education Funding Council for England (HEFCE) (1995) *Subject Overview Report: Geography*, HEFCE, Bristol. [Online] http://www.hefce.ac.uk/Pubs/ HEFCE/1995/qo_11_95.htm (accessed May 2002)

HEFCE (1998) *Evaluation of the Fund for the Development of Teaching and Learning* (98/68), HEFCE, CHEMS, Higher Education Consultancy Group, Department for Education Northern Ireland, Bristol

King, H (2000) Disseminating: theory and practice, *FDTL/TLTP Projects News Bulletin*, 4, pp 11–12

National Center for the Dissemination of Disability Research (NCDDR) (1996a) *Improving the Usefulness of Disability Research: A toolbox of dissemination strategies*, Guides to Improving Practice (no 2), NCDDR, Austin, Texas. [Online] http://www.ncddr.org/ du/products/guide2.html (accessed May 2002)

NCDDR (1996b) *Improving Links Between Research and Practice: Approaches to the effective dissemination of disability research*, Guides to Improving Practice (no 1), NCDDR, Austin, Texas. [Online] http://www.ncddr.org/du/products/guide1.html (accessed May 2002)

NCDDR (2001) *Developing an Effective Dissemination Plan*, NCDDR, Austin, Texas. [Online] http://www.ncddr.org/du/products/dissplan.html (accessed May 2002)

NCT (FDTL and TLTP National Coordination Team) (1999) *FDTL and TLTP Project Briefing no. 2: Dissemination*, FDTL/TLTP National Coordination Team, Milton Keynes. [Online] http://www.ncteam.ac.uk/resources/project_briefings/briefings/ brief02.pdf (accessed May 2002)

Westbrook, J D and Boethel, M (1995) *General Characteristics of Effective Dissemination and Utilization*, NCDDR, Austin, Texas. [Online] http://www.ncddr.org/du/ products/characteristics.html (accessed May 2002)

APPENDIX: GEOGRAPHY DISCIPLINE NETWORK GUIDES

Agnew, C and Elton, L (1998) *Lecturing in Geography*, Geography Discipline Network, Cheltenham

Birnie, J and Mason O'Connor, K (1998) *Practicals and Laboratory Work in Geography*, Geography Discipline Network, Cheltenham

Bradford, M and O'Connell, C (1998) *Assessment in Geography*, Geography Discipline Network, Cheltenham

Chalkley, B and Harwood, J (1998) *Transferable Skills and Work-based Learning in Geography*, Geography Discipline Network, Cheltenham

Clark, G and Wareham, T (1998) *Small-Group Teaching in Geography*, Geography Discipline Network, Cheltenham

Gardiner, V and D'Andrea, V (1998) *Teaching and Learning Issues and Managing Educational Change in Geography*, Geography Discipline Network, Cheltenham

Healey, M (1998) *Resource-Based Learning in Geography*, Geography Discipline Network, Cheltenham

Jenkins, A (1998) *Curriculum Design in Geography*, Geography Discipline Network, Cheltenham

Livingstone, I, Matthews, H and Castley, A (1998) *Fieldwork and Dissertations in Geography*, Geography Discipline Network, Cheltenham
Shepherd, I (1998) *Teaching and Learning Geography with Information and Communication Technologies*, Geography Discipline Network, Cheltenham

EDITORS' COMMENTARY

Phil Gravestock has explored a model of dissemination that uses an initial stage of dissemination for awareness. Many project managers struggle with this stage of dissemination because of the need to bring interested colleagues through awareness to a greater involvement with the work of the project.

Project GLAADH tackled this through a three-stage process. First, the project manager arranged for all art history departments in the UK and Northern Ireland to be interviewed. Conducting these interviews, and ensuring that at least the fact of the interview taking place (if not its content) was known in the department, achieved a good base-level of awareness about the project. Second, all interviewees were invited to a two-day workshop about the next stages of the project. Two-thirds of the interviewees attended the workshop. Third, out of this workshop, 10 development projects were identified from a range of very different institutions. It is hoped that, in this way, these 10 projects will be perhaps be disseminating to an already very receptive audience.

Project 'Real World' at Newcastle University tackled dissemination in a slightly different way. This FDTL Phase Three project, based in the Faculty of Agricultural and Biological Sciences, focuses on a generic topic, that of work-based learning. The project started with an open-invitation conference. From this conference the project team was able to shape a framework for work-related learning that was truly inclusive of the many approaches to learning both at and through work that were represented at the conference. This framework allowed the development of a practitioner network to harness practice in work-based learning across the country and beyond. As well as promoting the dissemination of practice, the network is further developing the work-based learning framework and supporting small development projects that have been identified through an open competition within their subject area. It will also provide the basis for dissemination for use, as the development projects begin to publish their work.

More and more projects have been collaborating on dissemination by running joint events such as workshops, seminars and conferences. At a time when academics and people working in commercial organizations have more pressure on their time and a greater choice of potentially useful events on offer, the combining of projects to provide a conference with broader appeal has potential benefit for all concerned. The delegates get a richer experience; the projects gain a wider potential audience, share the organization and costs and therefore reduce pressure on their time and resources.

For example, three projects with activities related to the built environment, RAPID, DEBS and Best Practice in Building Education collaborated on a one-day conference entitled Built Environment Education: Challenges for 2001 and Beyond. As well as presentations by the three projects, there was input by the Quality Assurance Agency and the LTSN Generic Centre. The combination of conference focus and the breadth of resources on offer, including other agencies, attracted over 60 delegates and was felt to have been a success by all three project teams.

9

Making an impact: the evaluation of History 2000

James Wisdom

INTRODUCTION

This chapter describes how the History 2000 project handled its evaluation dimension. The emphasis is on how the impact of the project was enhanced by integrating evaluation into the life of the project, rather than by attempting to use a research-based, quantitative approach which only tried to measure on closure day the overall change it had achieved. It describes how projects have a life and a growth of their own, how the context within which they operate is unstable and developing, and how an integrated evaluation process – by operating in the space between the project and its community – can help a project make its optimal impact in its specific and particular environment.

THE CONTEXT

History 2000, subtitled 'Developing reflective practice throughout the discipline', was the largest of the three history projects supported by the HEFCE's new Fund for the Development of Teaching and Learning (FDTL). It started in October 1996 and aimed to use the evidence of excellence which the Teaching Quality Assessment (TQA) had generated to help to improve the overall quality of history teaching. The other projects were Heritage Studies as Applied History (concerned with skills development arising from fieldwork in history, managed by Dr Simon Ditchfield at York University) and Assessment in Group Work (managed by Professor Roger Lloyd-Jones at Sheffield Hallam University). Details of these projects can be found through the Web site of the HEFCE Teaching Quality Enhancement Fund's National Coordination Team (www.ncteam.ac.uk).

History was one of the subjects chosen for the first round of the Higher Education Funding Council for England's new TQA process in 1993–94. Each history department prepared a self-assessment, and then a number of them were selected to be visited by small teams of historians who had put themselves forward to be trained to explore, disagree with or confirm those self-assessments. The departments selected were:

- all those that were claiming to be excellent;

- the ones where quality was deemed to be at risk; and

- a sample of those claiming to be satisfactory.

Evidence from the reports of the visits was used to create an overview of history provision (QAA, 1995) which reported that 89 self-assessments had been received, that student numbers in history had been rising rapidly in recent years, and that demand was still buoyant.

History is a major subject in British higher education, with many looking to old, prestigious universities (such as the large faculty of historians at Oxford) as the core of the profession. The History in the Universities Defence Group, an association of history lecturers, claimed (responding to proposals on the future of the Institute for Learning and Teaching) to be speaking for more than 100 history departments or subject groups, and 2,800 staff, who were teaching 33,000 full-time-equivalent students (1999). In the TQA, departments that were described as excellent tended to be those doing well in the Research Assessment Exercise (Brown, 1996; Booth and Hyland, 2000).

There was evidence of both success and difficulty in history teaching. It reported that history generally was taught well and that many examples of innovation in the curriculum, and lively and diverse teaching methods, had been found. However, 40 departments had had their claim for excellence rejected; some staff were burdened with heavy teaching loads; many staff saw modular programmes as an unfortunate but necessary dilution of the traditional preparation of a historian; increased student numbers had degraded the experience of seminars and diminished access to resources; and for many the 'skills agenda', with its challenge to traditional teaching and assessment methods, was seen as an unwarranted intrusion.

Paul Hyland (Bath Spa University College) and Alan Booth (University of Nottingham) had jointly edited *History in Higher Education: New directions in teaching and learning*. When they came to construct the History 2000 project, they chose to work from three central principles:

- The first was the recognition that the pleasures and difficulties of history teaching were common to many lecturers, and that there was much valuable experience and good practice throughout the community, in both pre- and post-1992 institutions.

- The second was the encouragement of reflection in reviewing current practice, with support for individual practitioners, for departments and possibly for the discipline as a whole.

- The third was the building of a community or network of colleagues who would look outwards, across and beyond their institutions.

For many historians, improving their teaching was not their most pressing concern, so perceptions were vital to the success of the project. It was important that it was not seen as the wholesale importation of new educational methods (which many saw as invasive and corrupting) nor as the comfortable endorsement of traditional practice. Disseminating existing good practice and using reflection with volunteers from the history profession was a good – perhaps the only – place to start.

FORMATION OF THE EVALUATION BOARD

The HEFCE circular, *Fund for the Development of Teaching and Learning* (1995), insisted that each bid show 'a clear strategy for monitoring the progress of the project and evaluating its success'. It also made clear that each project would be subject to periodic review which would trigger the phased payment of funds over the three years of the project.

In responding to the requirements of the invitation to bid, the applicants had laid out a monthly operational plan of tasks and achievable goals over the full three years. They could have chosen an evaluation strategy that was a process for monitoring monthly progress, delivering annual reports and, at the end, employing an external evaluator to report on the impact of the project as a whole. Or they could have appointed a steering group, though these bodies work best when they are in place from the beginning, engaged in the creation, design, steering, monitoring and evaluation until the end. The applicants selected a third approach.

The History 2000 project was designed to be run by a small team – two managers (Hyland and Booth) and the part-time administrator, Nicky Wilson. This team did not want to create a large, formal, impressive-on-paper advisory board, difficult to convene and perhaps distant from the project. They were looking for a small group that could be part of the team, to support them in a project which, in some respects, was unprecedented in history and for which success could not be guaranteed. So they appointed an 'Evaluation Board', inviting Professor George Brown (then at the

University of Ulster), Dr Jane Longmore (then Head of the History Department at St Mary's College, Twickenham), and James Wisdom (then Head of Educational and Staff Development at London Guildhall University). The board's formal brief was to receive reports from the team on each stage of the project, assess progress, and give advice and recommendations for future stages. These same reports were then submitted to the Funding Council for their regular reviews. The board also had a monitoring role (in educational terms, giving formative feedback) with a summative responsibility as the project ended. It also had a structural role, in that the papers supporting its eight meetings were the formal record of the project's history.

The board's informal brief was perhaps more important, and is best summarized as adopting the role of critical friend with elements of mentoring. A small board could do this more successfully than a large, more formal board. The project was run in a very open way, with all the main plans and papers being freely shared. Members of the Evaluation Board were able to participate in some events and did bring different perspectives and experiences to the project. Difficulties and disappointments were debated, not concealed. The Board was as committed to the success of the project as its progenitors, and because the atmosphere of the Board was informal, friendly and trusting, it was able to offer support for the heart as well as the head. Although historians may study change, they may not always wish to participate in it.

It is important to remember that the HEFCE had not established a research fund. FDTL was about the implementation of educational change. There would have been little point in finishing History 2000 with the words 'Well, that didn't work, but at least we know why.' The point is that projects aim for useful outcomes that will make a difference in the community, and so – during their lives – respond constantly to context and influences in order to do so. With additional funding, History 2000 ran for a fourth year, growing from its own experience and changing in response to significant developments in the educational world around it.

EVALUATION WITHIN HISTORY 2000

The primary focus of the Evaluation Board in the early months was to ensure that the project developed a culture of evaluation. This was perhaps easier in a project which focused on reflective practice than in other FDTL projects. Newsletters and flyers called 'Newslines' were published, a survey of good practice went out, and the programme of (individually evaluated) meetings, national seminars and departmental workshops got under way – all reported and reviewed when the board met. We learnt very quickly that lecturers wanted well-planned and practical sessions with plenty of opportunity for participation and discussion.

History 2000 was designed to support 12 one-year group projects in departments or between consortia, funded up to £10,000. The Evaluation Board participated in the process of deciding between the competing bids or restructuring them to more successfully achieve their purpose – it could bring a breadth of experience to these decisions. Foremost in all our concerns at this point was the need to overcome any perception that interest in learning and teaching was exclusively the preserve of the colleges and ex-polytechnics. The successful group project leaders knew that their proposals would be circulated to all history departments through the Newsletter, that they would be visited by the team during their project, that they would be expected to run both a seminar within their institution and a presentation at the conference, and to write a chapter for a new book. The culture of evaluation was deeply embedded within these projects.

The History 2000 team were vigorous in their delivery of the commitments made in their proposal. They held support meetings for project leaders, and national seminars on major issues in history teaching; published newsletters which reviewed history teaching, described the short projects and outlined the use of reflection; and started responding to the requests for visits to individual departments, either to act as consultants or to run workshops. The evaluation of these last against the national seminars showed that the local, bespoke work was more highly valued, and the project slightly shifted its practice in this direction. This was valuable for the project also, as it kept up an involvement with a wider range of staff than exclusively the enthusiasts.

For the main period of the project the emphasis of the Evaluation Board was on receiving reports, monitoring progress and maintaining the culture of evaluation. We were able to use informal as well as formal data to assess the project's direction and momentum: formal data comprised reviews of seminars and workshops, while informal data took the form of the growth in traffic – letters, e-mails and phone calls – between the project team and the community, requests for extra newsletters, and conference attendance from departments without a formal link to the project.

The board also tried to keep abreast of changes in the context around the project. Two external developments were important. The first was the HEFCE's creation of a National Co-ordination Team (NCT) to oversee the FDTL and the Teaching and Learning Technology projects. From early in 1997, History 2000 had access to the expertise of a national coordinator (Professor Graham Gibbs), more opportunities for contacts with the other projects, and an underpinning administration for managing the reporting process. Gradually the NCT would produce a wide range of briefing and guidance materials, drawing upon their own expertise and in response to

FDTL projects' needs and demands. The existence of the NCT diminished the need (never a prominent responsibility) for the Evaluation Board to act as an HEFCE auditor, enhanced the quality of advice and guidance the project received, and enabled the board to engage more with reviewing direction than examining detail.

The second development was the formation in 1997 by the Quality Assurance Agency (QAA) of a history subject group to establish a framework of national standards to be used by departments in a benchmarking process. This was part of a proposed new method of quality assurance, which was contested and debated by the sector as a whole. This debate had many effects, one in particular being an increased interest in what an improvement and enhancement project (such as History 2000) might be able to offer staff who were preparing for an assurance process.

One of the discussions in the Evaluation Board in the second year of the project was the difference between dissemination and implementation of educational good practice. Experience of other major programmes (in particular, the Teaching and Learning Technology Programme) showed that simply presenting products, processes, findings, good practice or outcomes to the academic community was not in itself sufficient to guarantee even an experimental uptake, let alone a full implementation. While the responsibility for encouraging or preventing change or even improvement in higher education practice can be shared by many elements, the position of head of department (or the equivalent role) is critically and strategically important. This was clearly emerging from the experience of running the programme of workshops and seminars. Therefore the History 2000 project team decided to set up a day for heads of departments, to brief them about the progress of the whole project and of the 12 group projects, and to prepare them for working successfully with colleagues enthusiastic to implement change.

EVALUATION OF HISTORY 2000

By the third year, starting in October 1998, the national context of History 2000 was changing. The QAA's reforms were being applied in Scotland, the Institute of Learning and Teaching was turning from an idea into firm proposals, and the HEFCE was developing a more comprehensive strategy for supporting educational enhancement work. One element of this was the formation of discipline-based services (called subject centres) which would be able to draw together the outputs of various projects and educational initiatives such as FDTL and TLTP. In addition, the HEFCE was offering additional funding to projects that were able to transfer their outcomes to new clients, or that could profitably be continued until the subject centre was able to pick up their outputs. Evaluation was no longer to be a summary act of completion (if it ever had been) – it was needed to support the further developmental work. The Evaluation Board now had a number of tasks.

Task one

The first was to review the whole process of supporting the short projects, particularly as this approach was being considered as part of the work of the subject centre. This was done through a workshop meeting between the three external members of the Board and the 12 group project managers, using a mixture of discussion, small-group work and individual reflection to look both back and forwards. Many of these projects had proved very effective and had been well supported. Their success lay in their size and in their short-term nature (one year of extra work and responsibility was as much as most leaders could afford if they were going to remain effective participants in the Research Assessment Exercise). The greatest anxiety arose from the need to present their outcomes in a way that met traditional standards of scholarly writing about educational practice and development.

Task two

The second task was to use the conference, held at Bath in April 1999, to evaluate the project. We ran three exercises:

- The first was to circulate and to listen. What were the 100 participants discussing? With genuine enthusiasm they were discussing the content of the sessions and how they might make use of the ideas.

- The second was to run a plenary session on the final day around the topic of 'what next?' In planning the future, historians would have to review the past.

- The third was to distribute a four-question feedback sheet, with plenty of space for the replies and comments. We took the view that it was too early for the precision of a numerical questionnaire.

We wanted to know:

- how respondents were involved with History 2000;
- how any work they might have done within a short project had affected their teaching, their department or their institution;

- what impact the programme had made on them and their colleagues;

- what they recommended for the future.

The replies were cross-referenced, aggregated and analysed, with individual quotations serving to exemplify the key points.

From all three conference sources we formed a clear view of a movement that was very conscious of being in its early stages, of individuals enjoying their enthusiasm but aware it was not widely shared, and of the vital need to support the tutors in the emerging network to the point where both they and the network as a whole could support departmental as well as personal change.

A thread running through all these evaluations was the importance placed on ensuring that staff from pre-1992 universities felt that History 2000 had as much to offer them as it did to the colleges and ex-polytechnic sector. The dangers of this division had been of particular concern when the applications to run or be part of the one-year projects had shown an under-representation from the pre-1992 universities. One example of usable data was the scrutiny of attendance at the three conferences and the three Heads of Department days. These showed that staff from the pre-1992 universities made up 40 per cent, then 45 per cent and then 53 per cent of the conference attendees (on an average attendance of 83). At the same time, the overall attendance at Heads' days was rising, from 40 through 75 to 79 (and the proportion of these attendees originating in pre-1992 universities remained between 43 per cent and 47 per cent). The proportion of workshops held in pre-1992 institutions grew rapidly in the later stages of the project.

Task three

The third task was to go beyond those who attended the conference to get some picture of how History 2000 – and the work it represented – was seen within the history community. Again, we were more interested in what this might tell the project about the planning for the prospective Subject Centre and other developments, than in making a summative judgement about success or failure. The project had not started with an estimation of how many historians it could affect, to what extent, and in what time span. Its designers knew their world well and were fully aware of how impervious some sections would be to the appearance of any public and self-critical discussion of teaching and learning. The key to the project was supporting self-reflection, not proclaiming a universal theory of best practice or advocating compulsory change. Given this approach, it would have been inappropriate (and impossible) for a formal evaluation process to have extended across the whole community. However, the overlapping networks that historians use did allow a widespread but informal process, through which well-placed members of the board made judgements about the impact, which in fact proved to be more positive than the overall external picture might have suggested.

Instead, however, we took a more focused approach, writing directly to a sample of users of the project with four open questions. We asked:

- what had been the best features of the project;

- whether it had been useful in developing teaching and learning in their department;

- what their key priorities were in teaching and learning for the immediate future;

- what advice we (the evaluators) should hear.

The replies confirmed the need to maintain the momentum and support the network, to keep up the flow of materials, ideas and discussion. Where departments had been developing an interest in some particular aspect of teaching and learning development, the opportunity for local workshops had been particularly significant. The way the whole project had been conducted – in both its openness of spirit and the strength of its administration – was especially important. In both this and the conference feedback there were examples of lecturers trying to link their work to other initiatives – benchmarking, teaching and learning strategies, departmental teaching development groups, the emerging subject centres, investment in information technology – to gain further strength.

There were also a number of opportunities to engage in other forms of evaluation that had not been planned into the original work programme, but that we could use to feed back into the project. The keynote papers given at the conferences by respected American historians and teachers (Professor Peter Stearns then at Carnegie Mellon University, Pennsylvania and Dr Peter Frederick of Wabash College, Indiana) were important opportunities to calibrate educational change in the UK against the ideas being developed in the United States. The process of editing, refereeing and publishing *The Practice of University Teaching* through the Manchester University Press was another exercise in calibration against demanding standards (Booth and Hyland, 2000). The invitation from the HEFCE to apply for further funding for a fourth year brought forward the summative evaluation, to inform the bid for continuation and transferability money.

In Spring 1998 the HEFCE had commissioned a full evaluation of the first two rounds of FDTL (including the National Co-ordination process), and History 2000 was one of the projects visited by the evaluation team.

The process of responding to and dealing with this enquiry was useful, and the report was published in November of that year as HEFCE 98/68, *Evaluation of the Fund for the Development of Teaching and Learning*. It drew particular attention to the importance and difficulties of effective dissemination, which History 2000 had attempted to tackle by emphasizing participation in educational change as the approach that most successfully ensured ownership. Finally, in November 1998 the project team conducted a full survey of the history community to support a response to the HEFCE's consultation paper on the formation of subject centres, and published it on their project Web site. In evaluation terms these were opportunities for triangulation (surveying from many points); in terms of the work of the Board in supporting a culture of evaluation throughout the whole project, they were ways of confirming alignment.

TOWARDS THE NEW CONTEXT

During the additionally funded year it was possible to see how articulation by the evaluation processes led to further developments of the main project. It had grown its community or network of colleagues, and their clear message was to keep the momentum. So it provided workshops on transferable skills and learning outcomes, a second successful conference for Heads of Department and a second national conference. Later, a training day for new history teachers was run under the auspices of the new Subject Centre. Again, there were examples of opportunistic evaluation to check on alignment (for example, using the Subject Centre's needs analysis across the whole community rather than focusing on another end-of-conference questionnaire), but the primary mechanism was to continue using the Evaluation Board to receive reports and make recommendations.

Informal evaluation was able to capture significant developments. The mood (to judge from the questions from the floor and the informal discussions) of the first Heads of Department conference was wary and cautious. It was concerned, among other things, with the politics behind the QAA's benchmarking process. A year later, despite some discomfort with the Institute of Learning and Teaching and the HEFCE's new Teaching and Learning Strategy documents, the mood of the second event was more relaxed and more confident. By the third such meeting – looking in particular at how to deal with the imminent reality of a new self-assessment and assurance process, and how to work with feedback, evaluation, difficulties and change in positive terms – there was a noticeable facility in the use of a shared language for discussing pedagogic concerns. It would not have been possible – in fact, it would have been counter-productive – to ascribe any such change in mood solely to History 2000, but it was in line with the original intention to support the development of a reflective community that could work with its own good practice and the use of outcomes from educational research.

What had been happening within the History 2000 project was a shifting of emphasis. In its early days, and in the early evaluations of workshops and conferences, the discussion was primarily around notions that there were ways in which individuals could improve their teaching; perhaps ideas could be drawn from other historians' experience, or from a generic literature applied within the historian's context? Reflective practice, action research, the classroom assessment techniques of Angelo and Cross (1993), evaluation guidance from George and Cowan (1999) and the networking and information exchange of History 2000 were available as structures to support the lecturer in his or her personal development. For many historians, however, there were issues of collaboration: for example, skills development frameworks (given extra emphasis in the work on benchmarking), curriculum design in a modular structure, best use of investment in information technology, and alignment of assessment methods (particularly of group work, seminar work and oral presentation). The project was able to accommodate these issues in its production of materials, in the outputs from the short projects and in the departmental consultancies and workshops.

At the same time the context was changing. In particular, the HEFCE was putting together a whole framework for Teaching Quality Enhancement and a funding mechanism to support it, which recognized that simultaneous action was needed on a number of fronts (individual, departmental, institutional and subject) to enable even some basic improvement work to happen, let alone to prepare for future developments (HEFCE, 1998, 1999). One part of this was the invitation to set up subject centres, and a measure of the effectiveness of History 2000 is that it had strengthened the discipline sufficiently for it to be able to respond creatively to that challenge. The project was able to grow to accommodate issues of departmental development within institutional strategies, and the management resources that were needed to support them. The network that it made available to the Subject Centre was therefore able to respond to the full range of improvement practices, from individual work with new and established staff, through supporting departments in reviewing their practice and underpinning the discipline's capacity to respond to the new quality assurance processes, to working with the opportunities presented by national developments in policy, strategy and funding.

CONCLUSIONS

The aim of History 2000 (from its final report to the HEFCE) was 'raising the quality of teaching and learning by stimulating, supporting and disseminating teachers' research, innovation and critical reflection on current practice'. It was beyond the resources of the Evaluation Board (and perhaps of the project itself) to have evaluated its success with students, by either opinion gathering or outcomes analysis. That was a responsibility for the teachers themselves (though it is now possible to see a role for the Subject Centre in supporting this work). Nor was it appropriate to evaluate its success with all teachers of history: the project had never adopted the evangelical approach of categorizing its colleagues as resistors, waverers, changers or champions. Nor would it have been particularly useful to engage only in a summative assessment as the project closed: the Funding Council, the National Co-ordination Team and particularly teachers in the discipline needed more than that.

What was clear, from the start, was that it was likely to be an evolving project within a rapidly developing context, and that evaluation needed to range from the formal, through the informal, to the opportunistic if it was going to generate the data and opinions that the team, and the other parties to the project, most needed. In the current environment of UK higher education, educational implementation projects are more likely to be dynamic than static. It turned out that a form of reflective practice – the core of the project – formed a stable foundation for the evaluation work as well.

REFERENCES

Angelo, T A and Cross, K P (1993) *Classroom Assessment Techniques: A handbook for college teachers*, 2nd edn, Jossey Bass, San Francisco

Booth, A and Hyland, P (2000) Introduction: developing scholarship in history teaching, in *The Practice of University History Teaching*, ed A Booth and P Hyland, Manchester University Press, Manchester, p 2

Brown, G (1996) Assessing the quality of education in history departments, in *History in Higher Education: New directions in teaching and learning*, ed A Booth and P Hyland, Blackwell, London, p 302

George, J and Cowan, J (1999) *A Handbook of Techniques for Formative Evaluation: Mapping the student's learning experience*, Kogan Page, London

Higher Education Funding Council for England (HEFCE) (1995) *Fund for the Development of Teaching and Learning*, 95/29, HEFCE, Bristol

HEFCE (1998) *Learning and Teaching: Strategy and funding proposals*, 98/40, HEFCE, Bristol

HEFCE (1999) *Learning and Teaching: Strategy and funding*, 99/26, HEFCE, Bristol

Quality Assurance Agency for Higher Education (QAA) (1995) *Subject Overview Report 3/95 – History*, QAA, Gloucester

FURTHER READING

Many of the documents discussed in this paper are available from the following Web sites:

- for newsletters and materials published by History 2000: www.bathspa.ac.uk/history2000

- for materials published by the History, Classics and Archaeology Subject Centre: www.hca.ltsn.ac.uk

- for the HEFCE circulars and invitations to bid: www.hefce.ac.uk

- for Fund for the Development of Teaching and Learning projects: www.nctcam.ac.uk

- for Quality Assurance Agency overviews and benchmarking standards: www.qaa.ac.uk

EDITORS' COMMENTARY

Widening Access to Experience Works is an Innovations project at the University of Newcastle. This project has three distinct streams, and the external evaluator identified very early in the life of the project that communications within the project team were not very effective. The external evaluator identified many opportunities for synergy between the three streams. However, because all communication was channelled through the project manager, these opportunities for synergy were missed. A more regular pattern of meetings was established. Some meetings dealt with the operational side of progressing the project, and others with academic integration and synergy.

The involvement of the external evaluator for this project was extended beyond the original time to allow him to review the success of the continuation strategy for the project. However, this project is not a mainstream activity of the Careers Service where it is based. Therefore the external evaluator is additionally being asked to draw up a business plan for this aspect of work of the Careers Service.

The Professional Integration Project based at the Royal College of Music had an evaluation strategy with two strands. The project was based in the discipline of music with all the project partners being music departments or conservatoires. It was vital to discover just how far the project had been successful within the discipline. However, professional integration – the development of professional skills and the integration of that development into the curriculum – is a topic that goes much wider than the subject of music. Just how transferable were the practices reported by this project, and the new ideas it generated? An external evaluator was employed who could go beyond the subject focus and assess the generic impact this project had achieved.

LUMEN chose to employ two different external evaluators simultaneously, to provide a broader overview of the project processes and outcomes. One, a subject specialist with a particular expertise in a core technological/pedagogical strand, was invited to focus on discipline-specific elements of the project. Most of his evaluation work was done towards the end of the project. The second evaluator was asked to begin at an earlier stage. He had experience of consultancy work both in relationships between HEIs and professional bodies, and in FE institutions. His evaluation focused on the processes and wider impact of the project (including a key dissemination event, a conference). The two evaluations complemented each other well and offered two alternative feedback perspectives to the project team at different stages of the project's life.

Evaluators are often used as part of the trials for a product – a piece of software or a new educational process – contributing to its development and improvement. The improved product, software or process is then published. This use of formative evaluation may be more familiar in a product development culture, but can still be appropriate in the context of evaluating an educational development project. One external evaluator noted in his final report that in the early days of the project his work was primarily formative, whereas towards the end his work was primarily summative.

The SAPHE evaluation report notes that it can be difficult to find hard-edged measurements when the project deliberately set out to explore the diversity of approaches to self-assessment, but that this difficulty of evaluation is in the nature of experimentation with education. This project was intended to develop people's thinking about the topic, and this is difficult to evaluate.

For many FDTL projects, evaluation of the workshops was a major part of the evaluation. The argument used was: 'We know the size of our community, we know how many of them have attended our workshops, we know how well the workshops went (because we had feedback forms at the end of every one), so we can make an estimate of the impact we have had on the community.' Then the difficulties start. How easily can the ideas generated in the workshops be disseminated to people who did not attend the workshops? How easily can those who did attend change their practice with their students? The reality is that the evaluation of workshops is form-ative and developmental, leading to change and growth in the project, but not a very useful way of measuring change in the community. However, they can contribute to a change in the culture, by encouraging familiarity with language and concepts.

Perhaps the most important thing for a project manager is to use the evaluator to ask questions in the wider context. It is very easy to get immersed in the detail of the project – 'How well are you doing the various stages that you have planned?' and so on – and much harder to keep facing the big questions about the community – 'How influential are you becoming?' The funding body is likely to conduct an external evaluation of the value of its programme. The project's external evaluator must ensure that when that happens, their project does not appear to be too far out of line. There can be a danger that a project is so inward looking that it thinks it is doing brilliantly while the rest of the world has not noticed that it exists, or has noticed but thinks it is doing badly.

10

Educational development projects in Australia: a system-level perspective

Richard Johnstone

BACKGROUND

It is now 10 years since a national body for the enhancement of teaching and learning in Australian universities was first established. The Committee for the Advancement of University Teaching (CAUT) came into existence in August 1992 with a brief both to help raise the status of teaching and to encourage higher-quality teaching and learning throughout the system. The creation of CAUT followed hard on the heels of a period of extensive restructuring in Australian higher education, a process that began in 1987 and extended into the early 1990s, leading in effect to the dismantling of the binary system. The formerly separate university and college sectors were combined, resulting in a quite different higher education landscape. In some cases former colleges of advanced education or institutes of technology became universities, either singly or by amalgamation, and in some cases former colleges were amalgamated with already established universities.

Among the many consequences of this period of intense activity was the emergence of a new focus on the central role of teaching and learning in the life of the university, and a new emphasis on the need to match their significance with that of research. In part this was a result of the introduction of new players into the world of universities, namely the colleges that had traditionally focused on teaching rather than research and brought that focus with them into the new and newly amalgamated institutions. It rapidly became clear, however, that neither of the formerly separate sectors had an advantage over the other when it came to the encouragement of a determined and strategic focus on the enhancement of teaching and learning. By far the most common approach across the board had been to assume a great deal about the quality of teaching that could not necessarily be borne out by rigorous investigation.

COMMITTEE FOR THE ADVANCEMENT OF UNIVERSITY TEACHING AND ITS SUCCESSORS

It was in this context that the Committee for the Advancement of University Teaching (CAUT) was established. This resulted largely from the work of several key figures in the university sector and the Commonwealth educational bureaucracy, and the impact upon their thinking of the establishment (in Sweden in 1990) of the Council for the Renewal of Undergraduate Education. The foundation chairman of CAUT, Dr Don Anderson, identified the committee's 'daunting task of helping to shift the culture of universities, which in the past few decades have become dominated by their research function, so that teaching is restored to its central position as the most important thing that university academics can do' (CAUT, 1994: iii). CAUT, supported by an annual budget of A\$4 million, established as its primary activity a system of nationally competitive teaching development grants.

In the reviews of, and commentaries on, the activities of CAUT (1992–96), together with its successor bodies – the Committee for University Teaching and Staff Development (CUTSD) (1997–99) and the Australian Universities' Teaching Committee (AUTC, see http://www.autc.gov.au) (from 2000) – a number of key issues emerge in relation to the management of projects and the achievement of successful outcomes. Certain commonly experienced problems or difficulties with project management and project completion have recurred. These include:

- initial underestimation of the scale of the task and the amount of work involved;

- lack of investment of both time and money in a continuous process of evaluation of the project;

- difficulty in sourcing appropriate project management skills and support;

- competing obligations of key project staff;

- difficulties in implementing project outcomes on a more secure, long-term basis.

The history of the three committees has to a large extent been the history of the identification of, and the varying responses to, these issues, in the light of both changing external factors, and mixed signals from the sector itself over the real value of central support for teaching and learning.

The role of individual and small-group grants

During the life of CAUT, 80 per cent of the available funding was devoted to the support of individual and small-group teaching development grants. These grants, awarded on a competitive basis to successful applicants from Australian universities, generally did not exceed A$50,000 in value. As the authors of the 1995 review of CAUT pointed out in their report, 'to put 80 per cent of its funding into support of individual projects and 15 per cent into all other activities (with another 5 per cent for administration) is a distribution which cries out for a public rationale and defence' (Moses and Johnson, 1995: 14).

The problem with providing such a rationale was that the strength of the underlying case varied considerably – as indeed it continues to do – according to the perspective taken. If, for example, the aim of the programme of individual grants was to generate cultural, structural and procedural change in universities, then the evidence for achieving that aim – while relying considerably on anecdotal and impressionistic evidence – was strong. Indeed, a theme that runs through the 1995 report into the activities of CAUT (and is echoed in the report of a review of CUTSD undertaken in 2000) is the confident identification, by a wide range of respondents, of a definite cultural change that took place in universities during the 1990s.

There is an almost universal belief expressed by respondents to the reviews that both CAUT and CUTSD have played a crucial role in:

- raising the status of teaching;

- providing recognition and reward to academics who focused on teaching;

- acting as a kind of template for the introduction of similar schemes within institutions.

It was not only teachers who felt this way. Most university academic administrators freely acknowledged the part played by these successive national committees in helping to drive the processes of recognizing good teaching at the faculty and institutional levels, particularly through the introduction of excellence in teaching awards and similar schemes, and by the revision of promotion criteria to highlight the value and importance of effective teaching.

Dissemination of good practice

If, however, another perspective is taken, that of the value of the individual project and its success in influencing practice more widely in the institution and the sector, then quite a different picture emerges. One of the key recommendations of the 1995 review of CAUT was in essence that CAUT redevelop two areas: a strategy for dissemination, and strategies for the adoption of good practice. The 're' in the word 'redevelop' continues to resonate in the light of the attempts by both of CAUT's successor committees to tackle and resolve the issues to which it refers. The review of CAUT identified a sentiment that was widely shared in the sector at the time, that notwithstanding the important role played by the system of nationally funded individual project grants in altering the cultural landscape, the other-than-local evidence for more concrete, practical and widespread outcomes in terms of improved teaching methods and improved quality of learning was less convincing.

Interestingly, in approaching this issue, the main focus has continued until recently to be on dissemination and its enemy, the so-called 'not invented here syndrome', rather than on the ways in which projects have been developed, managed and evaluated. It could be argued that this focus on dissemination, and on the encouragement of a culture of communication and cooperation across institutions has, in turn, been driven by the importance felt by successive committees of demonstrating above all else the value of the investment. The value had to be demonstrated not only to government, which provides the funds, but to those sceptics in the higher education sector who see those funds, however small a proportion of the overall higher education budget, as belonging by rights to the individual institutions rather than to a national body.

Both CAUT and CUTSD placed considerable emphasis on structures and programmes that would encourage effective dissemination of good practice, principally by means of sponsored workshops in the case of CAUT, and by annual National Teaching Forums in the case of CUTSD. In addition, CAUT, by means of a one-off allocation, established a set of 'clearing houses' that were designed to act as central points for the collection, evaluation and dissemination (largely by electronic means) of effective innovations in teaching and learning.

The difficulties experienced in the implementation of this scheme were attributable not so much to the clearing houses themselves as to some fundamental flaws in the ways in which they were established and overseen. There was a degree of confidence, which in hindsight seems misplaced, in the capacity of the clearing houses to attract by their own efforts the commitment and enthusiasm of the relevant university departments and faculties, without first ensuring commitment at the highest level from the universities themselves. More time could well have been spent in conveying to university management the advantages of the scheme, not least the potential advantages in helping individual institutions to both enhance quality and achieve economic efficiencies. Without that kind of imprimatur, the clearing houses were obliged to rely on their disciplinary networks, together with their own endorsement of successful innovations, to encourage active use of the resources they had gathered together.

In other words, there was a feeling that by identifying best practice, and making the examples of it easily accessible, then people would access these resources, and make effective use of them. The fact that this did not automatically happen was probably the single biggest influence in leading to a reconsideration of what was involved in effective dissemination and take-up, by focusing more squarely on the practical issues of effective project development and management.

The 1995 review of CAUT recognized the difficulties, but acknowledged that there were no easy or immediately apparent solutions. The report drew a distinction between dissemination and the adoption of ideas. It pointed out that 'good teaching practices and conditions for learning have been known in the broad, and in many specific examples, for many years. CAUT's challenge is to find ways of getting them widely adopted. Of course they have to be known in order to be adopted, but dissemination alone is not enough' (Moses and Johnson, 1995: 39).

A supportive constituency

It was also becoming clearer at this time that part of the problem associated with achieving effective dissemination was that the audience for such dissemination consisted largely of the converted, who in turn formed a kind of supportive constituency for a national focus on improving the quality of teaching. This would not in itself have been a problem had it been clear that the numbers of the converted were continuing to increase. On the contrary, however, it began to appear as if there was a kind of natural ceiling to the number of people who were prepared to focus on teaching and teaching innovation as a primary professional interest.

This is not to say that the 'unconverted' were not interested in or committed to good teaching, but rather to suggest that they may not have been prepared to adopt the language, the ethos, and what some of them may even have seen as the evangelical zeal of those of their colleagues who were actively involved in encouraging innovation by means of externally funded projects. That crucial gap between those occupying the charmed circle and those who preferred, for whatever reasons, to remain outside it was proving difficult to close.

The role of the early adopter

One factor working against the closing of this gap has been the somewhat mixed status in institutions of the so-called 'early adopter'. Ironically, the very success to which CAUT had contributed, of raising the status of teaching and of outstanding teachers, was also proving, to some extent at least, to be part of the problem. Instead of outstanding teachers being regarded as front-line generals whom the troops – partly out of admiration and partly out of a recognition that these generals were leading them in the right direction – would willingly follow, the early adopters and teaching innovators began in many cases to be regarded as the embodiment of an institutional commitment to the value of teaching and learning.

In other words, simply by existing, and continuing to achieve recognition and to garner awards, these outstanding individuals were often seen to be making their most important institutional contribution to teaching and learning. However, just as it was clear that there is a difference between someone who is an outstanding researcher and someone who is both an outstanding researcher and an effective research leader and manager, so it was becoming clear that something similar applies in teaching. The early adopters and outstanding innovators were clearly an institutional resource, but how best to deploy that resource was a difficult question.

COMMITTEE FOR UNIVERSITY TEACHING AND STAFF DEVELOPMENT

There was some doubt in 1996 whether the federal government would implement the first recommendation of the 1995 review of CAUT, namely that CAUT continue for at least a further three years with an increase in funding. It seemed, in a tight fiscal climate, and with a new focus by government on the student perspective on teaching and on a national system of course evaluation by recent graduates, that the initiative represented by CAUT, with its emphasis on teaching innovation, would fail to attract the necessary funds to continue. However, after some months of uncertainty, the Committee for University Teaching and Staff Development (CUTSD) was established, effective from the beginning of 1997, with a budget of A\$11 million over three years.

The new committee's objectives were to 'identify and promote good teaching, learning and assessment practices in universities; encourage and foster innovation in higher education teaching; and provide staff development opportunities for academic and administrative staff'. In responding to the 1995 review of CAUT, the new committee was concerned to address the issues identified as arising out of a primary focus on individual grants, and the related obstacles to effective adoption of project outcomes. At the same time members recognized the important role that nationally competitive individual grants had come to play in the life of individual institutions, not least in the authoritative role they had in validating teaching excellence.

The award and successful completion of a CAUT grant had become one of the most convincing ways for an individual teacher both to highlight the importance of his or her contribution to the university by way of teaching innovation, and to support any application for promotion on the grounds of teaching excellence. While many universities had by 1996 moved to establish their own internal system of competitive individual and small-group teaching development grants, many had not as yet done so, and national support for such grants continued to be seen by many people as a vital means of underpinning the value of the currency.

CUTSD, in its initial deliberations, was also aware that in addition to the many successfully completed projects, there were some that were being completed late or not at all. Some project leaders were also expressing frustration at the difficulties – caused by lack of time and funding – in taking their projects beyond what might be called the first stage, however successful in its own terms that first stage might have been. Part of the problem lay in recognizing that the successful completion of the project itself, according to the conditions and expectations under which it was funded, was in reality merely this 'first stage'. It is entirely understandable that the people actively engaged in the project would not see it that way. Typically they would be focused on achieving the proposed outcomes of the original proposal rather than on a long-term strategy of dissemination, a concept that was not in any case clearly defined.

Moreover, the members of CUTSD were aware of a significant communication gap between the committee itself (including its predecessor CAUT), which was responsible for assessing project proposals and distributing funding, and both prospective and successful grant applicants. The aims and priorities of the national committee were not necessarily being communicated effectively, and by the same token the teachers themselves did not have a clear mechanism for communicating with the committee. A network of CUTSD Liaison Officers, representing each university, was established to facilitate communication and in particular to provide feedback to CUTSD on issues of concern in the sector. The CUTSD Liaison Officers identified the lack of emphasis or institutional expertise in two key areas, project management and project evaluation, as one of the more significant obstacles in the way of ensuring timely and effective completions.

Ensuring effective project management and the adoption of outcomes

With the benefit of hindsight, it is apparent that the identified gap in project management skills was not directly addressed by the CUTSD committee, but rather served as a background against which certain key decisions were taken. Moreover, the intuitive causal connection that was made by members of CUTSD – by which effective project management would increase the chances of wider implementation beyond the life of the project – was not interrogated as robustly as it could have been. Debate tended to focus instead on the question of whether the typical size of the individual grants as awarded by CAUT was sufficient to ensure effective outcomes and wider implementation.

In this context, CUTSD approved a reduction in support to the category of individual and small-group grants, and the creation of a new category of organizational grants. At the same time it continued to administer a programme of staff development grants that had formerly been the responsibility of a separate national Staff Development Committee. Members reasoned that only by offering academics the opportunity to bid for larger grants – up to A$200,000 in value – were these projects likely to achieve a critical mass that would ensure both a longer life for the project and a wider impact. The revised selection and assessment criteria for project applications highlighted the crucial role of ongoing project management and reporting. At the same time, inter-departmental and inter-institutional collaboration in these organizational grants, while not mandated, was strongly encouraged.

By involving a range of participants from the very beginning of a project, it was hoped to achieve a 'buy in' by those participants who would ensure broad take-up of the outcomes. Indeed this priority, of encouraging wide participation in the development of project applications (preferably involving several different universities), reflected the conviction of CUTSD members that commitment to the deployment of project outcomes was set very early in the process, at the time of developing the grant application. To attempt to achieve that level of commitment at the end of the project, from colleagues in other institutions who had not been previously involved, was recognized by CUTSD, on the basis of the experience of CAUT, as a very daunting exercise.

In creating the new category of organizational grant, CUTSD predicted it would lead to a steady drift of applications away from the individual and small-group category towards the greater flexibility and opportunity offered by the organizational grants. This proved to be only partly true. The overall number of applications for small grants did decline, as anticipated, but so did the number of applications for the new organizational grants, from an initial peak of 93 in 1997 to 87 in 1999. In part this represented the increasing demands being placed on academic staff, and in particular on the teaching innovators most likely to have the necessary credibility as project leaders, but an additional factor may have been the difficulties involved in drawing together a consortium of equally committed participants from institutions often located at great distances from one another.

REVIEW OF CUTSD

A review of the activities of CUTSD, as yet unpublished, was undertaken in 2000 by Allan Schofield of the UK Higher Education Consultancy Group with the assistance of Alan Olsen of Kuringai Consultants, Sydney. This indicates that, overall, organizational grants were effective in contributing positively to institutional practice. It was, however, equally clear that, notwithstanding the increasing emphasis placed by the committee over the three years from 1997 to 1999 on the importance of cross-institutional collaboration, the impact on the wider sector had not been by any means as strong. Among the important reasons for this disappointing level of impact, Schofield and Olsen identified an inability on the part of CUTSD to follow through with the level of support it would ideally have liked to have been able to offer. This was seen in part as a result of the difficulty in securing high-level professional staff to assume leadership roles. Schofield and Olsen concluded that responsibility for system-wide support and dissemination consequently fell upon committee members who were already heavily committed elsewhere.

AUSTRALIAN UNIVERSITIES TEACHING COMMITTEE

Under the influence of comments such as these, CUTSD began in 1999 to look closely at the UK experience, and particularly to the nature of the professional support provided at the national level both to projects in development and to continuing projects. Towards the end of CUTSD's three-year term there was once again some uncertainty as to whether a national teaching body of the kind represented by CAUT and then CUTSD would continue. The Minister for Education and Youth Affairs announced the creation of a new body, the Australian Universities' Teaching Committee (AUTC), effective from the beginning of 2000. The new committee was initially established for two years, with its term of office subsequently being extended until the end of 2002.

Once again the new committee, like CUTSD before it, was in the position of receiving a report about its predecessor, and using that report as a basis for determining future directions. Limited funding made a competitive system of grants difficult to maintain at the necessary level, but there were other factors that led AUTC to adopt a significantly different direction. After eight years, a large body of work in the form of completed projects had been accumulated. Many of these projects were successful in their own terms, but had fallen into abeyance. Essentially this was because the resources and indeed the skills required to take them beyond their funded life and exploit their full potential were not available, either at the national level or from the hard-pressed budgets of individual institutions.

Taking into account the available funding, the priority for AUTC was to invite expressions of interest in undertaking discipline- and theme-based projects. The terms of reference of the AUTC encouraged investigation of the ways in which issues of teaching and learning have been approached at the disciplinary level, in the context of various factors such as: the increasing impact of the new technologies and of globalization; the changing student body and student expectations; and variations over time in the work graduates are doing, and the work employers want done.

In effect, the new committee felt that the time had come to review what had been achieved to date under its predecessors, and to draw out from the examples of successful or potentially successful innovation those aspects that had the greatest capacity to impact positively on teaching and learning practice within the particular discipline.

In seeking to identify examples of best practice in teaching and learning in Australian universities at the level of discipline or field of study, the AUTC highlighted the different natures of the disciplines, and the ways in which effective innovation is frequently a response to the particular circumstances and pedagogical requirements that apply at the disciplinary level. This represented a significant departure from previous thinking: it recognized the crucial role of disciplinary and professional networks in ensuring effective take-up of best practice.

More importantly, AUTC modified the hitherto standard approach adopted by its two predecessor committees, of allowing the competitive process itself to decide the areas on which the funded projects would focus. Unlike CAUT or CUTSD, the AUTC initiated a process of itself developing project briefs, often to quite specific levels of detail, and calling for expressions of interest to undertake the projects described in those briefs. The selection process then focused on identifying respondents who would be invited to develop fuller proposals in a further round, again in line with the project brief developed by CUTSD. Although it was not described as such, this approach can be seen as being a response to the acknowledged need for more effective project management, greater linking of objectives and outcomes, and more clearly identified impact.

Grants of between A$150,000 and A$300,000 have been made in disciplinary areas such as business and law, and in key thematic areas such as the applications of information and communication technology, and in assessment. The AUTC did not, however, have the resources at its disposal to implement one of its preferred aims, a national unit or secretariat, staffed by teaching and learning professionals, that would provide counsel and assistance to all projects in areas such as management and evaluation.

Faced with its inability to fund such an initiative the committee, as an alternative, established a set of project-specific steering groups that would oversee the projects and would sit between the project leaders and the AUTC, ensuring effective liaison between them. Each steering group is chaired by a member of the AUTC, and comprises roughly equal numbers of university and external members. The role of the steering group is to monitor progress, to provide advice, and perhaps most importantly to identify and keep abreast of problems as they arise. If necessary, it is the role of the steering group to advise AUTC if a project is not meeting its stated aims and needs to be discontinued.

In establishing a form of committee structure – rather than an operational unit – to deal with issues of project management, the AUTC, partly but not entirely for financial reasons, has followed a theme that characterizes the practices of all three committees, namely a reliance on volunteer contributions from the sector to ensure the effective operation of the granting process. In a climate in which increasing demands are made on the staff of universities, one of the more difficult questions to answer is the extent to which that sense of professional obligation and commitment, on which committees such as the AUTC depend for their effective operation, can continue to be relied upon.

CONCLUSIONS

In reflecting on the experience of CAUT and CUTSD, and the initial years of the AUTC, it is apparent that issues of project management, and in particular the role played by effective management in laying the ground for dissemination, have been a primary focus of all three committees. If a trend can be detected, it has been a movement away from a reliance on small-scale individual projects, through to larger, more collaborative ones, and most recently to projects that involve a considerable component of central direction in the project brief. The overall impact of this trend has been to complicate rather than simplify the business of project management.

The larger and more collaborative the project, and the more specific the outcomes required by the funding body, the more crucial and complex become the issues surrounding project management. One of the most noticeable outcomes of this trend is that experience or track record has become more and more highly valued by the project assessors. In that sense the emphasis has shifted dramatically in 10 years, from supporting the university teacher and one or two colleagues in trying out a good idea, to a culture of grant giving that favours the experts over the enthusiasts.

To some extent of course it has been those early, individual grants that have created the experts, and given them the 'on the ground' experience to tackle larger projects. In a sense, the definition of 'project' has also changed, and with it the skills required of a project manager. The focus now is not so much on the development of new ways of teaching and learning, as on the identification of existing examples of successful innovation, and on the ways and means of ensuring their continuing and widespread implementation.

REFERENCES

CAUT (1994) *Annual Report 1992/93*, Australian Government Publishing Service, Canberra
Moses, I and Johnson, R (1995) *Review of the Committee for the Advancement of University Teaching*, Australian Government Publishing Service, Canberra

11

Project management in educational development: a Singapore experience

Tan Oon Seng

INTRODUCTION

In the early 1990s the broader scenario for higher education development in this part of the world was one of confidence and investment in education. In the mid-1990s East Asia was often hailed as a region of rapid economic growth (Naisbitt, 1996). The world trends in educational development for developing countries indicated rapid expansion of educational systems and enrolments at all levels (Singh, 1991). The *Asian Economic Survey* (1994) in a special report entitled *Can Asia Keep it Up?* noted, however, that in the longer term there were many issues of concern. These included structural changes in governments' business policies, environment policies, infrastructure developments and education.

The advent of unprecedented technological developments, globalization and economic developments have important implications. Many involved in large- or small-scale educational projects hoped to jump-start and accelerate development with promises of resources, information superhighways, quick replication through collaboration, and so on. In Asia education, allied to the work ethic, is seen as a passport to wealth and development. Educational development projects are thus accorded some priority and are usually recognized and taken seriously.

How effective are educational projects and initiatives in this part of the world? Harvard-trained and highly experienced World Bank consultant, Dr Chai Hon Chan told me that in his 20-plus years of experience and observation of many large-scale educational development projects, funding and resources were not the primary problems. The greatest problem was the lack of project management skills, especially in developing countries, resulting in the failure to absorb good practices and successful implementation of ideas.

Project management skills are often taken for granted. Sadly, people do not learn from the lessons of success and failures in projects. Following the 1998 Asian economic crisis and the more recent world recession, the resources available for educational development projects have dwindled as governments and funding bodies have trimmed budgets. Project management skills have become even more important in ensuring that whatever is invested results in fruitful long-term outcomes.

SOME HIGHER EDUCATION TRENDS

In a keynote address on 'World trends in higher education: the Singapore and Southeast Asian context', I noted (Tan, 1996) that higher education in the 1990s was characterized by the following concerns:

- development in teaching quality;

- educational quality assurance and funding policies;

- impact of increased opportunities in education;

- impact of technology and knowledge explosion;

- changing societal expectations, industrial and business demands;

- benchmarking, niches of excellence and strategic planning.

The types of educational development project in which I had been involved include: initiating a compulsory, internationally accredited, Teaching in Higher Education certificate programme for new academic staff; establishing an educational quality assurance system; total quality management initiatives; a national human resource development system known as 'The People Developer'; a Thinking Initiative Programme; and finally an institution-wide implementation of problem-based learning. My situation was unique in that I was then in a newly established tertiary institution and was involved in many development and change initiatives pertaining to education and staff development.

What do I mean when I refer to 'projects'? A project entails a clear goal with a deliverable outcome. Usually by a project we refer to work that has a beginning and an end rather than processes or routine work that are ongoing. By an educational development project I refer to work that aims to create change in specific aspects of education. An educational development project involves an articulation of the objective and educational benefits that it hopes to bring. There are also clear descriptions of the rationale, scope, resources and time frame, how it will be accomplished and how we are going to monitor the development and evaluate its achievement. We can characterize educational projects as involving the following phases:

- the context: pre-planning, positioning and definition;
- organization and planning;
- implementation and monitoring;
- review.

The above are probably stereotypical stages for most projects. For educational development projects, it is often difficult to define the 'completion' stage, as such projects are aimed at spearheading a change process that is meant to be ongoing. Nevertheless, completion can be delimited, usually in terms of (1) a time frame within which to measure desired outcomes, or (2) the duration of funding. What is most important, however, is understanding the critical factors that ensure success in each of the above stages and hence bring about effective change.

In this chapter a case study of an education innovation is used to highlight the experiences along each of the stages of the project in the context of an Asian culture – that of Singapore. While there is cross-cultural validity in some of the broader principles of effective project management, I hope to highlight some of the lessons and insights that can be gained from looking at factors peculiar to educational development, as well as those pertaining to cultural factors where relevant. The nature of educational development projects makes them rather different from a project, say, on an institution's physical structure or its information technology infrastructure. Cultural factors pertaining to areas will also be discussed, such as the way we deal with planning, the management of uncertainties, people issues, motivational factors and the management of resistance.

THE CONTEXT

As it is a small global city with one of the best IT infrastructures in the world, the dynamism, proximity and intensity of change is easily felt in Singapore. The call for curriculum innovation in Singapore has been featured in a report entitled *Committee on Singapore Competitiveness* (Ministry of Trade and Industry, 1998). The report stated that, in order to improve the long-term competitiveness of Singapore, there is a need to refine the education system 'to help foster creative thinking and entrepreneurial spirit among the young' (Ministry of Trade and Industry, 1998: 86). It argued that three major components of the educational system should be addressed, namely, the content of the educational curriculum, the mode of delivering this curriculum to students and the assessment of students' performance. The Ministry of Education (1998), in a booklet entitled *The Desired Outcomes of Education*, also included the following as goals of post-secondary and tertiary education:

- being innovative;

- having a spirit of continual improvement;

- a lifelong habit of learning;

- an enterprising spirit in undertakings.

Indeed, the challenge for educators is to design new learning environments and curricula that really encourage motivation and independence, in order to equip students with the learning and problem-solving skills and competencies that employers are looking for. In a university survey of employers' rating of important skills, the top eight items in order of importance were: team work, problem solving, ability to take initiative, desire to learn, interpersonal skills, ability to work independently, oral communication and flexibility in applying knowledge (National University of Singapore, 2000).

What kinds of educational development projects would respond to these changes? Educational innovation has never been easy, whether it has involved incremental changes in curricula or the implementation of alternatives to existing practices (Ford, 1987). Pockets of innovations that are initiated from the ground usually do not last very long. In this part of the world most projects have generally been top-down, as resources have tended to be given for global and clearly structured projects.

Projects do not always end on a positive note. Huberman (1989) and Little (1996) observed that more often than not staff involved in institution-wide innovation are disenchanted at the end of such projects. Furthermore, while the rationale for proposed changes is often taken to be sufficient, Swann and Pratt (1999) noted that there is a tendency for the research underpinning them to be less than satisfactory.

As Morrison noted, 'whilst one can plan for change in a careful way, in practice the plan seldom unfolds in the ways anticipated' (Morrison, 1998: 15). Morrison observed that 'evolutionary planning' works better then 'linear planning'. The idea of curricular innovation at Temasek Polytechnic did not happen overnight. As a staff developer at the polytechnic, I saw a need for curricular innovation in terms of moving away from the traditional lecture–tutorial approach to a more learner-centred and active learning approach. I had noted (Tan, 1994), in my research on how lecturers designed a curriculum, that little attention was given to the needs of the learner and what learners would be empowered to do. Using the model of Oliva (1992) about the consideration (that is, planning time) given to (1) the learner, (2) society, and (3) the subject matter, I found in a survey of academic staff (with 65 respondents) that only 27 per cent of staff gave high ratings for seriously considering the learner as the most important focus. However, 65.4 per cent rated highly the amount of consideration given to the subject matter. These findings were consistent with Ramsden's (1992) view that the needs of learners and how they learn had not been given sufficient attention. I argued for the need to 'create opportunities for students to commit themselves to a learning task and learn by doing' and further noted that 'what is probably more important is the need for case studies, problem-based learning and simulations of real-life situations' (see Chong, 1995: 3).

On the basis of these macro-developments the initiative for a problem-based learning approach to polytechnic education was conceived, which resulted in the eventual setting up of the Temasek Centre for Problem-based Learning (PBL). The centre was set up 'to meet the challenges of preparing students for the world of dynamic change' by adopting 'a new academic architecture' that featured problem-based learning (Tan, 2000a, 2000b). It was envisaged that PBL would benefit students in terms of developing problem-solving acumen, integrated knowledge-based learning, and lifelong learning. Through PBL, students were expected to attain greater self-motivation, develop higher-order thinking skills, and team work and communication skills (Albanese and Mitchell, 1993; Boud and Feletti, 1997; Tan *et al*, 2000).

The centre serviced the polytechnic by providing opportunities for staff to be trained in PBL through workshops, forums, open lectures and exchanges with PBL experts. Through the centre, the academic staff of the polytechnic were exposed to workshops which included: Introduction to PBL, Design of PBL Problems, Facilitation in PBL, Curriculum Development in PBL and Assessment in PBL. Selected staff from the polytechnic were sent to various international PBL centres such as those at the University of Southern Illinois, University of Maastricht, University of Newcastle (Australia), University of Samford and the Illinois Mathematics and Science Academy. The centre also provided consultation to the various schools of the polytechnic (namely, Design, Business, Engineering, Information Technology and Applied Science) to help with both curriculum development for, and research and development in, PBL. The centre also acted in collaboration with the local and international centres to exchange and advance the practice of PBL. One of the accomplishments of the centre was the hosting of the 2nd Asia-Pacific Conference on Problem-based Learning, which saw over 140 paper presentations and some 500 local and overseas delegates.

I must mention a few pointers at this stage. Educational development projects are concerned with bringing about change and meeting needs. Positioning is an important aspect of such projects and in order for it to be effective it is necessary to note the following considerations.

- **Global trends**: you need to be aware of global and regional trends that may be related to what you want to do. This will help you rationalize and articulate your project.

- **National agenda**: be very cognisant of national agendas and priorities, not only to be politically correct but, more importantly, because a project at the micro-level or a small project that is fulfilling a particular national priority can actually take off much faster than top-down initiatives.

- **Know the state of the art**: we commit to a project to advance good practice or a field of knowledge, and we take a stand that whatever changes in policies may happen we intend to work on it because our loyalty is one of improving a particular practice in a field we are committed to.

- **Commitment to change**: an educational development project in particular is about a commitment to change underpinned by sound educational beliefs or philosophy.

- **Beyond educational justification**: look for more than just educational justification. Previous educational research does not necessarily convince people. Multi-pronged justifications such as those pertaining to economics and social impact help.

- **Action research**: do your own action research and preliminary surveys to support what you want to do.

- **Consistent championship**: consistently champion and advance a good idea over a period of time. Projects do not just happen with a one-off idea.

- **Build a team of people**: project teams can be formed by assignment, but when you have a collaboration between a group of like-minded people it is much easier for things to take off.

- **Collaborative international network**: having a network of people locally and internationally who share the same interests can be very helpful even though they may not be part of the project team.

ORGANIZATION AND PLANNING

At Temasek Polytechnic there were many initiatives for interactive approaches to enhance learning, and mini-projects, pilot projects and some action research projects were also taking place. Many of these initiatives originated from individual staff or groups of staff who were intrinsically motivated to characterize their courses with not only unique professional content but unique learning approaches. Some of these initiatives were facilitated by the staff development unit. One requirement for the formalized staff development programmes was an assignment that represents a non-routine contribution to teaching and learning. Owing to its inception as a new institution, the bulk of Temasek's staff were recruited from business and industry and, as such, most new staff had to undergo the compulsory Teaching in Higher Education certificate programme. The staff were expected to adopt predominantly innovative, rather than traditional, modes of teaching and learning.

Concomitant with the search for a more active learning methodology was increased awareness of the need for change. The viability of a traditional lecture–tutorial system with heavy emphasis on content knowledge has been seriously questioned, but pockets of interactive learning seem to satisfy neither staff nor students. Active learning was emphasized with a view to enhancing thinking, and to combining higher-order thinking skills with creativity.

One initiative that caught the attention of management and staff developers was a pilot programme by a team of computer engineering staff. They came across the concept of problem-based learning and picked up further expertise through study trips and training at the University of Southern Illinois. They adapted the PBL approach developed there in medicine, and applied it with enthusiasm to their computer engineering programme. The project caught the attention of the principal of the polytechnic, who immediately saw the potential of using PBL across more courses. As I was heading the Thinking Initiative Programme (which actually preceded the Temasek Centre for PBL) as well as the staff development unit, I saw that PBL philosophy and pedagogy could usefully anchor curriculum innovation. The challenge then was about nurturing the idea and growing it into a major project. We seriously needed a project to facilitate further developments, fan into flame the sparks of action, spread the fire to management, and help staff who were challenging the status quo and who were trying to promote a shift in the way we look at teaching and learning. The presence of some like-minded PBL champions, with the passion and commitment necessary to put this innovation into practice, was an opportunity that needed to be seized and exploited.

The kind of paradigm shift that is required in order to implement PBL

What is important is a shift towards designing more real-world problems, as anchors around which students can achieve the required learning outcomes in the process of actively solving unstructured problems. I argued that by using a 'real life' problem (rather than the subject content) as a focus, students would really learn how to learn: they would take the role of active problem solvers, and their teachers the role of coaches. It was postulated that in this way the learning paradigm would shift towards the attainment of higher-level thinking skills (Tan, 2000b; Tan *et al*, 2000).

I was privileged to see the implementation of PBL in a context where the administration and management gave full support and advocated the use of PBL as the anchoring philosophy for professional training and education. The piloting and implementation also won national recognition when a number of colleagues and I won a S$176,000 'Innovator Award' for co-pioneering PBL as an innovation in education. What we celebrated about the award was not so much our initiatives as educators but the fact that the Enterprise Challenge Award from the Prime Minister's Office had recognized educational innovation – problem-based learning – as part of a S$10 million Initiative (the only one out of seven awards to be in education).

On reflection I note two major milestones that epitomize the importance of looking out for, and seizing, opportunities so that a project can be strategically positioned and be implemented. The first involved an organizational-level strategic planning session where a management retreat was held to 're-invent' polytechnic education. This led to a search for a new academic architecture. The second was the recognition from this national body, The Enterprise Challenge (TEC). The TEC grant of S$176,000 was to be used to fully pilot PBL in one of the business courses. It was a 10-month intensive project to develop a prototypical curriculum with templates for course development, facilitators' and learners' packages, assessment and comprehensive evaluation. The intention was to focus, define and delimit the scope of the project, so that it could be evaluated.

Educational development projects, unlike industrial or management projects, tend not to have a clear boundary and are often multi-faceted. By choosing just one course it was easy to articulate the scope, resources, timeline and realistic deliverables. It was also important to know clearly what the funding body wanted. In the case of the TEC award I had to appear before a final panel that comprised the Permanent Secretary of the Ministry of Manpower, chief executives from the public and private sectors, and senior staff from the Office of the Prime Minister. I had to focus on three things: originality, feasibility and benefits. I was selling a new educational paradigm. I remember being asked what was so original about the idea of problem-based learning. My argument was that it was a revolutionary rather than evolutionary approach to professional education. It was novel because we intended to have an entire curriculum revamp that would change the way we dealt with content, the mode of delivery, the role of the lecturer, the activities of the students and the mode of assessment. I made sure I also limited the project to an area where feasibility and benefits were realizable.

Some of the key lessons pertaining to organization and planning educational development projects can be summarized as follows:

- **Conviction and clarity of purpose**: a strong conviction and clear idea of what you want to change helps provide the meaning and motivation without which there would be little momentum for organization and planning.

- **Well-developed ideas and mental models**: it takes time to develop an idea, formulate it in mental models and communicate it.

- **Visualize the feasibility and benefits**: it helps in project planning to have the end in mind and to visualize the outcomes and benefits.

- **Systems thinking and systematic thinking**: planning and organization involve a constant awareness of the holistic aspect of the project as well as of the detailed planning.

Singapore is well known for its efficiency in many spheres of government, public and commercial services, and work. Education is no exception, and generally projects are well organized and planned. During the development of a project there is usually high commitment from, and involvement of, the appropriate people, good use of focus groups, quality check points and review of progress. Thus in our project the teams were clearly organized with roles and responsibilities defined. Major milestones were established with clear timelines and control and monitoring mechanisms.

IMPLEMENTATION AND MONITORING

While a culture of strong planning, systems thinking and systematic thinking helps provide the foundation for projects to be started effectively, the tasks of implementation and sustaining momentum are never easy.

What are the major obstacles? The first pertains to dealing with paradigms and mindsets. PBL involves a rather radical change, and while its philosophy and rationale seem convincing, people are highly sceptical as they do not know how it will work in practice. The Temasek Centre for Problem-based Learning provided staff development in areas of PBL design, facilitation, curriculum development and assessment. Furthermore, course teams embarking on PBL worked with PBL staff as they developed their curricula. It should be noted, however, that PBL was new to both staff developers and teaching staff. Major skills gaps were experienced in the areas of curriculum design, facilitation and assessment.

The other obstacles were related to existing systems and processes. While top-management support may be given, there are often bulky systems which have been in place a long time, and which need to be changed. PBL innovation requires breaking barriers in many academic policies and systems. For example, the Programme Validation Committee and the Senate have to be consulted when major curriculum changes and changes in modes of assessment are involved. Going through these major committees meant that things would be slowed down tremendously. There were also the Education Quality Assurance systems, which used standard student feedback forms designed to assess the effectiveness of lectures and tutorials. The lecturers' roles in PBL were very different, so the standard student feedback form still included things like 'clarity of explanation', whereas PBL entails getting students to seek and obtain their own solutions or explanations.

The approach we adopted, however, was one of educating peers and helping them become informed. Because the case here won national recognition, it therefore has strong negotiating influence. Nevertheless, great acknowledgement of the large intertwining systems was still essential, and building collaboration and giving ownership were critical.

The completion of the TEC project, and other pilot projects, was defined in terms of a full cycle of PBL implementation for a particular academic year. (Incidentally, the institution also employs total quality management extensively.)

Owing to the fact that PBL was prescribed as a useful alternative to traditional pedagogic methods, surveys of lecturers' perceptions were generally positive. Nevertheless, surveys and monitoring of student feedback produced mixed results. While quantitative data were helpful in obtaining a broad picture, the most valuable sources of insights were qualitative. In an situation where PBL is implemented institution-wide, what are students saying? I think the very people who are the focus of PBL can help us gain insights into how PBL has empowered them, or perhaps created helplessness in them. Are students finding more meaning or direction with PBL, or are they perhaps more lost than they would have been under traditional teaching methods? Does PBL meet students' needs? Does PBL redefine students' needs in such a way that empowers them for the future?

Some student reactions to PBL

Student A

I think the problems were very helpful because they kept us focused on thinking [about] the learning issues and the solutions. Even when we were not using the library or checking the net we continued thinking about them. My lecturer taught us to use lateral thinking, so, because we had been working on the problem, we sometimes got new ideas from thinking about other things, not necessarily in the subject area.

Student B

I think through PBL we really become better in problem solving. We learn to clarify our assumptions and concepts. We also ask more 'why' questions and apply logical, critical and creative thinking at various stages. I learn that one has to flexible rather than be fixed in a particular mindset. ... Yes, I think the tutor plays an important role in helping us develop problem-solving skills in PBL.

Student C

I am just a very average student and I find that I am sometimes very slow in understanding the lecture-type courses. Once I can't follow I get more and more lost. In PBL, however, I can learn at my own pace. I can tell my group members that I don't get it and they will explain it to me. Sometimes I really try hard to read [and] I still cannot get it, but the other members know my difficulty and will take time to explain to me.

Student D

Doing PBL is like solving a jigsaw puzzle, but it is frustrating because we are not given any big picture, not even the scope, in the beginning ... it is like giving us a few jigsaw pieces and asking us to find the rest of the pieces. The worst thing is that at the end of everything I still don't get an overall picture.

Student E

The PBL tutorial process doesn't work. ... We don't really like the tutor. She is very businesslike and assumes that we have all the time to work on the problem. We know that she is against 'spoon-feeding' and that she has a good knowledge herself, but we hope she can understand what we are going through. She [could] give us more encouragement and guidance. Sometimes in our group discussion when we

> are working up to a certain point which is quite critical, all we need is
> just a bit of hint or something … or someone to tell us if we are going
> in the right direction, but we can only consult the tutor at certain
> specific times and even then [it seems there are] a lot of things we are
> not supposed to ask!

Whitehill, Stokes and MacKinnon (1997) observed that PBL was developed
in the West and may face problems of 'cultural transportability'. It is a
familiar fact that PBL begins with a problem and uses problems as the
anchors for motivation and learning. The power of problems, however, has
not been optimized in many PBL courses. The design of problems poses a
major challenge for PBL educators. It appears that the best problems are
those that we obtain from industry and other real-world contexts. The
implication here is that problem designers need to get into the real world
to document and collect a repertoire of such problems. This is not easy,
given the administrative constraints and multifaceted roles of academic
staff today. It points, though, to the need for the institution to re-examine
its concepts of staff development and industrial attachment. It also calls for
new strategies of partnership between institutions and industry.

Review
The power of a real-world problem is obvious from the vignettes, but it is
important, when presenting a real-world problem, that the context is well
presented. There are conflicting experiences of students and lecturers
about the theoretical conceptions of PBL. There appears, for example, to
be a need for a scaffolding of relevant information to be presented. Not
enough attention has been given to ensuring a good closure. Owing to the
emphasis given to process, in most cases closure tends to be concerned with
providing opportunities for students to share their reflections of how they
have been doing as problem solvers, and their evaluation of their participation as team members.

We have, as a result, been relatively neglectful of how we look at the
knowledge we have been dealing with during the PBL process. There was a
chasm between advocates of so-called 'pure' or 'authentic' PBL (Barrows,
1988) and the reality of students' experience. There are those who claim
that PBL need not activate one's prior knowledge and that we could start
with a problem in a domain totally unfamiliar to students. It appears that in
practice there are many instances where this assumption is questionable.
PBL is not an all-encompassing approach to learning.

The vignettes also illustrate the experience, or at least the perceptions,
of students in the PBL tutorial process and the quality of their interactions

with tutors in PBL classrooms. In our experience the lecturer as a coach is a major factor in the effectiveness of PBL courses. The vignettes seem to raise some questions such as the following. What really is the role of the tutor? What are the characteristics of effective facilitators or coaches? What skills do tutors need to have in order to ensure that students benefit from the PBL process? How well are academic staff coaching and empowering students in the process?

While PBL is about learner centredness, the role of the lecturer as facilitator is by no means passive (Albanese, 2000; Tan, 2000b). PBL does not just take place as a consequence of being given a good problem, a well-designed schedule, resources, and the necessary opportunities for small-group learning. The experiences of the students quoted above appear to point directly to tutors' failure in process facilitation. Woods (2000) noted that one of the most challenging tasks in PBL is the development of process skills. He argued that both previous research and experience point to the fact that many process skills such as change management, team work, conflict resolution and problem solving do not just happen because students work in small groups. This calls for staff to be (1) equipped with competencies of process skills (handling group dynamics, questioning skills, facilitating meta-cognition and so on), and (2) able to identify, articulate and assess these skills. From the vignettes the PBL project on the whole appears promising in addressing several of the intended outcomes, such as catering to individual differences in learning and empowering independent learning, the ability to get information and learning how to learn. PBL also appears to be a good approach to learning interdependence and socialization. It is also evident that PBL as perceived by students has potency in bringing them closer to real-world experiences.

From the perspective of educational development project management, what insights and lessons can we draw from a review of the processes, interactions and outcomes?

The uncertainty principle

In a culture where planning and systematic thinking prevail, the very strength of project planning becomes a major weakness. I learnt the hard way to propagate what we may call the uncertainty principle of project management. When we try to locate where we are on the timeline of project completion we are often unsure about the momentum, about how and where it is heading and with what intensity! Thus in PBL all we know is that we are practising things characteristic of PBL, but we are really not so sure whether we are achieving some of the intended outcomes. Even systems of evaluation have to be changed because we are not measuring the same things as previously. The example given was student feedback. Accepting the uncertainty principle is a necessary part of project management and, in particular, of educational project management.

Practical and systems barriers

The experiences with this project point to the fact that de-skilling and re-skilling are essential to practise PBL. The lack of PBL skills was one factor responsible for many of the implementation problems. There were many other practical problems that were related to one another, including the lack of resources such as time, administrative support, space and materials. In spite of all the planning, PBL resources for students, the design of problems, availability of rooms for PBL-type discussions and support staff were often lacking at one time or another. Sometimes staff were caught in a vicious cycle where the lack of time, support and resources led to poor quality from stage to stage.

Furthermore, the systems in place did not support change. In fact, the more efficient the current system, the greater it is as a barrier to change. Thus if the educational quality assurance system has been developed and fine-tuned over a period of time for a lecture–tutorial based system, it is not easy to disband the system quickly to cater for the PBL approach. Yet the quality system will inevitably be tied to staff appraisal systems and course evaluation systems.

Clearly, a single project of educational change is not normally conceived with immediate consideration for existing systems. The only solution is one of flexibility on the part of the custodians of these systems, and it is here that project leaders have to win collaboration and promote ownership of new ideas through strategic communication.

Mindset and value barriers

The PBL project involved mindset change in academic staff and students as well as administration. People naturally feel more secure, comfortable and confident with familiar of ways of teaching and learning, and changes are bound to be resisted initially. Staff training and plenty of preparation were needed to overcome individuals' psychological barriers. There are also cultural barriers which are sometimes difficult to penetrate. In issues of teaching and learning, cultural barriers pertaining to value and belief systems go deeper than individuals' psychological barriers. This is especially difficult in Asian cultures, where people are disinclined to articulate strongly held beliefs and personal philosophies about the way learning should be done. Resistance sometimes results in paying lip service or 'conspiracy of the least', namely, doing enough just to get by. There are no easy solutions to such resistance; the positive approach is to establish niches of success to showcase and convince people of the true value and benefit of the project. This is why the idea of recruiting champions for a project is crucial to a project's success.

The whole is more than the sum of its parts

The PBL project experienced student resistance in the initial stages of implementation. If we had relied on initial responses alone to decide whether or not to proceed, the project would never have taken off. Similarly, there were many parts of the PBL experience that were not optimized when the changeover was taking place. The holistic approach and systems perspective that we took were helpful in addressing the various problems that cropped up.

EPILOGUE

As Laufer and Hoffman observed, 'all work is project work' (Laufer and Hoffman, 2000: xi). Given today's dynamic developments in higher education, almost all aspects of our work and work roles are challenged with change in different directions. All project work is about change initiatives. Educational projects in particular are delimited by time frames and funding for various administrative reasons and constraints. Nevertheless, educational development projects – more than other kinds of project – are iterative in nature and spiral in development. The same processes have often to be revisited, and the outcomes are but the beginning of another iterative process. A reflection on some of the critical successful factors discussed in this chapter points to the fact that many of these factors transcend all cultural and national boundaries. Good management of educational development projects, it appears, is about championing a desired change that is rooted in well-informed deliberations and planning. It is about challenging the status quo and taking risks by being cognizant of both the global developments and localized contexts. While the technicalities of planning, scheduling, resource allocation, prioritizing and so on are important, the factors that make it work are people, collaboration and ownership. The capacity for flexibility and human networking is often needed to transcend systems and procedures.

REFERENCES

Albanese, M (2000) Problem-based learning: why curricula are likely to show little effect on knowledge and clinical skills, *Medical Education*, **34**, pp 729–38

Albanese, M A and Mitchell, S (1993) Problem-based learning: a review of literature on its outcomes and implementation issues, *Academic Medicine*, **68**, pp 52–80

Asian Economic Survey (1994) Asian Economic Survey: Can Asia keep up? *Asian Wall Street Journal*, Hong Kong

Barrows, H (1988) *The Tutorial Process*, Southern Illinois University School of Medicine, Springfield, Illinois

Boud, D and Feletti, G I (1997) *The Challenge of Problem Based Learning*, Kogan Page, London

Chong, E (1995) *Recess: Education the next wave*, Temasek Polytechnic, Singapore

Ford, S (1987) *Evaluating Educational Innovation*, Croom Helm, New York

Huberman, M (1989) The professional life cycle of teachers, *Teachers College Record*, **91**, pp 31–57

Laufer, A and Hoffman, E J (2000) *Project Management Success Stories*, Wiley, Toronto

Little, J W (1996) The emotional contours and career trajectories of (disappointed) reform enthusiasts, Cambridge Journal of Education, **26** (3), pp 345–59

Ministry of Education (1998) *The Desired Outcomes of Education*, Ministry of Education, Singapore

Ministry of Trade and Industry (1998) *Committee on Singapore Competitiveness*, Ministry of Trade and Industry, Singapore.

Morrison, K (1998) *Management Theories for Educational Change*, Paul Chapman, London

Naisbitt, J (1996) *Megatrends Asia: Eight Asian megatrends that are reshaping our world*, Simon and Schuster, New York

National University of Singapore (2000) Selected results from 2 CDTL Survey, *CDLTLink*, **4** (2), National University of Singapore Centre for Development of Teaching and Learning

Oliva, P F (1992) *Developing the Curriculum*, 3rd edn, Harper-Collins, New York

Ramsden, P (1992) *Learning to Teach in Higher Education*, Routledge, New York

Singh, R R (1991) *Education for the Twenty-First Century: Asia-Pacific perspectives*, UNESCO Principal Office for Asia and the Pacific, Bangkok

Swann, J and Pratt, J (eds) (1999) *Improving Education: Realist approaches to method and research*, Cassell, New York

Tan, O S (1994) Curriculum development for the 21st century: a model and perspective for course designers, *Temasek Journal*, July

Tan, O S (1996) World trends in higher education: the Singapore and Southeast Asian context, in *Waves of Change* (extended abstracts of 7th National Conference of the International Student Advisers' Network of Australia), ed G Sanderson, pp 21–24, Flinders Press, Australia

Tan, O S (2000a) Reflecting on innovating the academic architecture for the 21st century, *Educational Developments*, **1** (2), pp 8–11

Tan O S (2000b) Intelligence enhancement and cognitive coaching in problem-based learning, in *TLHE Symposium Proceedings*, ed C M Wang, K P Mohanan, D Pan and Y S Chee, pp 167–72, National University of Singapore

Tan, O S, Little, P, Hee, S Y and Conway, J (2000) (eds) *Problem-Based Learning: Educational innovation across disciplines*, Temasek Centre for Problem-based Learning, Singapore

Whitehill, T L, Stokes, S F and MacKinnon, M M (1997) Problem-based learning and the Chinese learner, in *Learning and Teaching in Higher Education: Advancing international perspectives*, ed R Murray-Harvey and H C Silins, pp 129–46, Higher Education Research and Development Society of Australasia, Australia

Woods, D R (2000) Helping your students gain the most from PBL, in *Problem-based Learning: Educational innovation across disciplines*, ed O S Tan, P Little, S Y Hee and J Conway, pp 12–36, Temasek Centre for Problem-based Learning, Singapore

12

Learning from educational development projects

David Baume

INTRODUCTION

Many of the chapters in this book describe educational development projects undertaken in UK higher education. Others look more widely, to project work undertaken in Australia and in Singapore. This chapter looks more widely still, at a number of projects undertaken in various countries (including the UK). The projects discussed in this chapter have all been described in the pages of the *International Journal for Academic Development* (*IJAD*). *IJAD* is the journal of the International Consortium for Educational Development (ICED). ICED was established in 1995 to link together national educational networks and to encourage and support the growth of new networks. More details about *IJAD* and about ICED and its member national networks can be found on their respective Web sites (see http://www.queensu.ca/idc/ijad/ and http://www.edu.yorku.ca/ progers/iced/).

Few of the papers discussing these educational development projects give much explicit attention to issues of project management, being much more concerned with academic and conceptual issues, with data and its understanding and with emergent theory. This relatively low attention given to project management issues is in itself interesting. A thesis of this book is that explicit and thoughtful attention to the management of an educational development project is necessary for the success of the project. However, a discovery from reading journal papers through the lens of project management is that project management has not generally been seen as worthy of explicit academic analysis by educational developers.

Although it is possible to gain, from reading the papers, a wealth of information about approaches to the management of educational development projects, it has been necessary – as well as fascinating – to dig for the information. An additional benefit from this chapter may be that it will help readers to find information and ideas about the management of educational development projects, even in accounts of such projects that do not give much explicit attention to project management.

The bulk of this chapter works from paper to paper, describing for each one the major issue or issues in project management, drawing implications for practice from each paper. These implications are considered further in a concluding section.

Fewer than one-tenth of the papers published in *IJAD* are considered in this chapter. Four main criteria were adopted in the selection of papers for the production of case studies here:

- the accessibility, directly or by clear inference, of information on project management issues in the paper;

- a range of countries of origin;

- a range of types of projects;

- a range of scale of projects.

PROJECT MANAGEMENT ISSUES ARISING FROM THE PAPERS

Attending to context

Establishing a new educational development unit would match most developers' conceptions of a 'project'. Sue Johnston and Di Adams (1996) from the University of Canberra, Australia, stress the importance, for the success of the project, of attention to context.

One context to which the authors of the paper refer is the existence in the great majority of Australian universities of an educational development unit, albeit differing somewhat in structure and roles. The existence of many other such units, the associated group of educational development professionals, and the associated professional groupings, conferences and publications, together provide a positive context, access to peer support and some (though not total) shared meaning of 'educational development' and 'educational development unit.'

Implication: Find and use your peer support group(s).

A second context is the particular agenda that the unit was set up to serve, in this case a growing national concern with quality assurance for teaching and learning and, fortunately, a related (and at the time well-funded) concern for quality enhancement. (The authors comment that 'In many respects, the quality agenda has provided fertile ground for the work of educational development units' (Johnston and Adams, 1996: 20). By similar token the requirement that each English university should produce a Learning and Teaching Strategy has stimulated much development work in English universities.)

Implication: Identify and align with national priorities.

A third context is the particular institution in which the unit was to be established, and its particular concerns and values, in this case 'a relatively small Australian university by Australian standards with some 9,000 students' committed in the words of its mission to 'educating professionals, professionally' (Johnston and Adams, 1996: 21). The new unit was to be a vehicle for achieving this.

Implication: Identify and align with institutional priorities.

A fourth context was the perception by the staff of the unit, informed by their reading of the institution, of the 'need for the unit to prove itself of worth to the university very quickly and effectively' (Johnston and Adams, 1996: 21) through a full programme of events, publicity, visits, services, projects and contributions to policy.

Implication: Anticipate and overcome in advance possible institutional concerns.

There are other valuable lessons for the management of a project in this paper, including: the need, not just for the design of any educational development project to play close attention to the many different contexts in which it needs to function, but also to ensure that its plans and methods give weight to the many, varied and sometimes conflicting needs of those contexts; the need for 'quick wins', for an educational development project to prove itself quickly; the need for political skills.

Attending to disciplinary demands

Alan Jenkins (1996) from Oxford Brookes University, UK, describes his 'academic journey from a long period of teaching and researching geography to recently taking on the role of an educational developer'. To summarize his very thoughtful paper, he describes his strongly held view of the central importance of discipline to the practice of academic development. At the start of the paper he quotes with approval Lee Schulman's observation that 'the key to understanding the knowledge base of teaching lies at the intersection of content and pedagogy', and draws many implications from this powerful statement for the practice of academic development. (I cheerfully acknowledge the profound and lasting effect that this paper by Alan Jenkins has had on my own thinking and practice as an academic developer.)

Implication: The paper has a clear message – academic development work and projects must give substantial and sustained attention to the issues of the teaching of the discipline. Generic approaches by contrast may be less effective.

There is a need for further work, conceptual and experimental, to refine this view, and to identify when and how educational development projects can address generic teaching and learning issues as well as subject-specific issues. But in the meanwhile, Alan Jenkins' plea for attention to the discipline remains good advice for any educational development project.

Sensitivity

Deniz Gokcora (1996) from Portland State University, Oregon, United States, describes a study into a potentially fraught topic. Teaching Assistants (TAs) from the People's Republic of China 'constitute 30 percent of the TA population in the US' (Gokcora, 1996: 34). The study investigated the perceptions held by Chinese TAs and American undergraduates of what makes a good teacher. The differences identified were related to the different views of education held by the two groups – 'Chinese value content, Americans tend to value presentation'. The main method used in the study was focus groups, of TAs (at various stages of progression through a programme on teaching) and of American undergraduates.

Implication: I learn from this paper that, with appropriate respect for cultural difference and with a sensitive research approach, projects can safely and productively investigate and draw implications for action in what may at first hearing appear to be very difficult and sensitive areas.

Holding dreams, attending to reality

Peggy Nightingale (1996) describes the externally funded design and clearly successful introduction of a programme of three courses – graduate certificate, graduate diploma and Masters – on university teaching at the University of New South Wales, Australia. Peggy Nightingale then comments: 'The only problem with trying to be inspirational is that various realities intrude – the reality of operating within a large bureaucratic system with resource constraints, and the reality that both teachers and students are human.' She then goes on to say 'Six years of experience have driven home some uncomfortable learning experiences for the teaching team.'

The experienced project manager may sigh on reading this; the new project manager may become fearful. They may wonder what particular realities have intruded here, what might have been done in advance to mitigate them or afterwards to overcome them. They may also wonder which of these or similar realities may be about to intrude into the reader's own project. Peggy Nightingale's honest and thoughtful, if somewhat depressing, account is very valuable.

The first realities are the cost and both the academic and administrative workload involved in running a Masters degree in an academic centre that also has many other duties. The administrative workload was all the greater because the centre had to create the infrastructure for running courses.

Implications: Development projects by their nature tend to do new and different things. Developers by temperament tend to be optimists, concerned to innovate, to dream and implement those dreams. They may also, perhaps, be unable or unwilling to see the scepticism of others. It may well be that no one has done exactly what your new development project will do; but the odds are that someone has done something in some ways similar. At the planning stage, identify development projects that have some similarities with yours, ask to see the project plans and reports, talk to the project director or manager and ask him or her what he/she did, how well it worked, and what he/she wishes had been done differently. The managers and staff of development projects are generally keen to share experience.

The second realities is the need to compromise with ideals. University regulations about courses, and assessment and completion schedules, were not compatible with the hopes of the course team to run a strongly participant-centred programme. However, the course team, with strong support from the Higher Degree Committee, was sometimes able to negotiate compromises. And sometimes university regulations and requirements were found, in the light of experience, to be helpful rather than the hindrance they were at first thought to be.

Implications: Seek early clarity about the framework of rules and procedures within which the project must operate. Fit in with these as far as you can. If any of the rules or procedures really will seriously distort or damage the work of the project, then, perhaps through one of the project's champions, seek to negotiate changes to or exemptions from those rules or procedures. (Going somewhat beyond the paper, you can sometimes negotiate exemptions from current procedures on the basis that you will conduct a pilot or trial of a modified procedure, and of course evaluate and report back.)

The third realities are the 'uncomfortably complex and ambiguous role relationships' (Nightingale, 1996: 47) between the participants on the programme (academic staff who are subject teachers) and the teachers on the programme (academic staff who are academic developers). To take just one stark example, programme participants are peers of those who deliver the programme, and at the same time are subject to their judgement, to being assessed by them, perhaps with implications for their tenure and progression, and certainly with implications for their self-esteem.

Implication: Multiple role-relations such as those that Peggy Nightingale describes are an inevitable feature of life in a complex organization. Those who are managing projects need to anticipate such situations. For example, a project manager may in some settings need to direct the work of a senior academic. Such 'complex and ambiguous role relationships' need to be acknowledged openly, and reviewed and discussed. This may defuse some difficulties before they arise.

Working on a large scale with several supporting factors

Many educational development projects use, and indeed rely on, dissemination to enthusiasts and volunteers rather than to the entire potential population of users. Marie-Louise Schreurs and colleagues at Maastricht University, The Netherlands, devised a staff development programme for all experienced teaching staff in the Faculty of Health Sciences at the university (Schreurs, Robertson and Bouhuijs, 1999). The subject of the programme was teaching through problem-based learning (PBL), the predominant teaching method in the faculty.

The staff developers who devised and ran the programme felt that 'a necessary condition for the successful implementation of a large-scale faculty development programme like this is a supportive attitude of the faculty board' (Schreurs *et al*, 1999: 117). In fact several factors were acting in support of the initiative: external funding, some of which was used to 'buy out' teaching staff time to allow them to attend the programme; the active support of the Dean; and the knowledge that consideration would be given to participation in training when later decisions were made about tenure and promotion.

The project team took many steps to ensure participation. A project team was formed including key senior faculty staff, reporting to the faculty board. To respond to staff reservations about the programme, information about the programme was widely shared, and the programme was emphasized as providing chances to share experience, rather than as being remedial in intent. The Dean chaired an initial meeting of the programme, and allowed time for questions and discussion. Programme topics were chosen after an analysis of the skill requirements for teaching through PBL. Programme workshops were explicitly informal, and based on an explicit model of change process. Participants were encouraged to choose workshops that addressed their particular current concerns. During the workshops, participants produced and planned teaching materials for their future use, rather than just talking about issues and practice. Each workshop was evaluated. Over the two years of the project, 60 per cent of the 180 or so staff eligible took part in at least one event. The authors compare this figure with data showing participation elsewhere in faculty development by only some 5 per cent of tenured staff each year, a comparison they find encouraging to their project.

Implications: Attaining a high degree of participation in a development event or process requires active consideration of each of the many factors that can encourage or discourage participation. In planning a project with ambitious goals for dissemination and reach, it is worth making an effort to identify at least the major success factors, and then planning to maximize each of these factors. Particular success factors may include:

- adequate funding, for the project and for buying out staff time;

- ensuring support at all levels through consultation and continued attention;

- clear needs analysis;

- for a training course, ensuring the immediate practical applicability by participants both of the content of the training, and of the development work undertaken by participants during the training; and

- continuing evaluation and consequent changes to process.

Grounding in theory

Every educational development project has a basis of theory or belief. This basis may not be articulated, but it is always there. Examples are: 'This goal (the goal of the project) is attainable'; 'The goal of the project is worth attaining'; 'The intended methods will successfully and cost-effectively lead to the attainment of the goal.' Staff development projects, too, embody theories, about what will prompt and support academics to review and change their practices. However, it is unusual to develop a staff development programme explicitly on the basis of a theory about staff learning. Angela Ho (2000) from Hong Kong Polytechnic University describes the development of such a programme.

Angela Ho starts with the recognition that 'university teachers hold personal conceptions that are related to their teaching practices and also to the learning of their students. This has led to the recognition that genuine improvement in teachers has to begin with a change in their thinking about teaching and learning itself' (Ho, 2000: 31). From this starting point, and from detailed consideration of the literature on how teachers change their conceptions, she designed a staff development programme which aimed to bring to the surface, first, teachers' current conceptions about teaching and learning (their espoused theories), and second, the conceptions that were implicit in their practice (their theories in action). The programme aimed then to identify any inconsistencies between their two sets of views about teaching and learning, to offer different theories about teaching and learning, to help teachers formulate revised conceptions about teaching and learning, to work out implications of these for their practice as teachers, and finally to help teachers to commit to adopting appropriate new approaches.

Evaluation of the programme showed: changes in the conceptions of teaching held by a majority of participants; changes in practice made only by those whose conceptions of teaching changed; and, for half the teachers who changed their conceptions, positive effects on the approaches to learning adopted by students.

Implication: An explicit theory or theoretical orientation can form a sound basis for an educational development project and also for evaluation of that project.

Negotiating goals and process

Barbara Grant of the University of Auckland, New Zealand and Sally Knowles of Murdoch University, Western Australia were concerned to help academic women to become academic writers. They saw some of their concerns as practical: helping colleagues to start to write, to increase productivity and satisfaction in writing, and to get published. Behind these, they saw deeper concerns: for example, about how academic women do and do not understand themselves to be writers. They describe the long route, familiar to many people who devise an educational development project, from a broad area of interest or concern, to detailed analysis of need, to appropriate practical action and its evaluation (Grant and Knowles, 2000).

Barbara Grant and Sally Knowles's project was a five-day live-in writing retreat. There was an explicit and non-negotiable outcome from the event: the production of an article for publication, or another chapter for a PhD thesis, as appropriate. This was to be a writing event, not just an event about writing. Accepting this outcome, the participants negotiated a programme: one seminar each day on an agreed topic (after lunch), two work in progress seminars (each evening), and lots of quiet writing time. Evaluations were very positive; most resultant papers were completed, and some published; the retreats have been repeated; the community of participants has expanded.

Implications: The 'project' of the writing retreat sprang from the authors' consideration – personal and academic – of the issues of women as academic writers over a number of years. The overall goal of the event was clear and non-negotiable. This goal was also both attractive and defensible to the participants, who had to commit to the project and who had to justify their expenditure of time and money. Within the non-negotiable overall goal, the process itself was negotiated, within a fixed frame of time and venue. The project thus had a solid academic and personal grounding, a clear and attractive goal, and a negotiated process. These qualities will contribute to the success of many an educational development project.

Consulting to achieve embedding

Janice Smith from the University of North London, England and Martin Oliver from University College London, England (Smith and Oliver, 2000) describe a three-year, nationally funded project, EFFECTS (for Effective Framework For Embedding Communications and Information Technology using Targeted Support). The aim was to develop and accredit the capabilities of academics who use learning technologies in their teaching.

There are many possible ways to achieve this. Rather than starting with the design of training courses and materials, the project started at the end, with an account of the seven generic learning outcomes of an EFFECTS programme. (Briefly, these outcomes are: reviewing the use of learning technologies; selecting appropriate learning technologies; planning the integration into practice of appropriate learning technologies; doing so strategically; evaluating impact; disseminating findings; and undertaking one's own continuing professional development – all underpinned by an understanding of the underlying educational processes.)

This account was developed and refined through a long process of consultation with higher education institutions. Institutions were then free to develop a course or programme to meet their particular institutional needs, and receive national accreditation for it. (This is very similar to the approach implemented in 1992 by the UK Staff and Educational Development Association (SEDA) to the accreditation of programmes for the accreditation of teachers in higher education (see Baume and Baume, 1996), and the SEDA Web site www.seda.ac.uk. The EFFECTS framework is formally recognized by SEDA.)

Implications: Successful embedding of an innovation requires ownership by those adopting the innovation. First, EFFECTS has shown that long and thorough consultation is an effective way to generate such ownership by the user community. Second, EFFECTS has shown that a simple and clear framework, in this case a qualification framework, defines and helps the achievement of a common standard, while freeing those involved to meet particular local requirements. A third implication of EFFECTS for successful embedding is that the project needs to be clear about what should be tightly specified and what should be left to local interpretation.

Negotiation and consultation; clarity over outcomes and principles; freedom as to local interpretation and implementation. These are three good guidelines for developers working in higher education. Academics value their freedom!

CONCLUSIONS AND SUGGESTIONS

The following overall conclusions and suggestions for the planning and management of staff and educational development projects arose from my reading of the papers referred to. Additional conclusions may of course be drawn. *IJAD* proved a useful source of ideas about the management of staff and educational development projects. The methodology of this chapter – the mining of published papers for insights into project management – can be applied both to other *IJAD* papers and, of course, more widely. These insights will need to be tested for their applicability in your own project and setting.

Context

All educational development projects take place within a particular context and culture. Most take place within many: within a local institution, department or school, programme or course, each with its own policies and priorities; within a particular national higher education system, each again with its own concerns; and in one or more disciplinary or professional contexts. It is valuable in the early stages of planning a project to identify, explicitly, the main relevant contexts, and then to explore how features of each of these contexts can provide both sources of support to be exploited, and obstacles to be anticipated and mitigated or overcome. Some adaptation and compromise from original project goals and methods may well be appropriate.

Discipline

The academic discipline(s) with which the project is to work is a sufficiently important contextual factor to deserve particular attention. There are limits, as yet not well understood, to the effectiveness that generic educational development projects can have on practice within the disciplines, and thus to what can be achieved by educational developers working in an a-disciplinary way. If the outcomes of a project are intended to have effect within a defined discipline(s), then members of that discipline should be involved in planning, undertaking and disseminating the results of the project. If the outcomes are intended to be applicable across all disciplines, then staff from at least a sample of disciplines should be involved.

Ownership

Academics are much more likely to adopt, adapt and implement an innovation in their teaching and learning work if they have had some stake in its creation. The widest feasible consultation, on the original project specification and then on successive iterations of the project, develops this ownership and hence increases the chance of adoption.

Success factors

What would really make the project fly? What could damage or ground it? Identify the answers to these questions near the start of project planning. Return to the questions at each stage of project review, and be prepared to see new or revised answers. Check whether the success factors are still being delivered and the failure factors avoided, and act accordingly.

Change plans and goals

Adapt to changing circumstances. It is a poor idea to stick with a plan that is no longer working properly. It is equally a poor idea to stick with goals that, as a result of changed circumstances, are no longer appropriate or optimal. It is usually advisable to negotiate such changes of plan or goal with the project sponsor.

Relationships

Members of a project team may well have more than one professional relationship with each other and with project participants and clients. The most obvious of these might be peer, manager and assessor-evaluator. Explicit attention to and management of such different relationships can reduce the scope for friction and discomfort.

Peers and networks

There is fast growing experience in the planning and operation of educational development projects. Conversations with people who have run other projects will identify their learning, and will thus help you to make fewer, or at any rate different, mistakes. Most educational developers are reasonably friendly and approachable – it's the only way they survive. Connect with local and national networks of developers and project staff.

Framework

Educational development projects are often undertaken in a somewhat a-theoretical way, which is understandable given the relatively low (but fortunately fast growing) theoretical base available for educational development. Theories and models from related disciplines – such as education, management, psychology, and organizational development – can offer scaffolding on which to build projects. The use of an explicit basis in one or more theories or models can aid the development and analysis of project plans, and the evaluation of project outcomes. Hopefully you will develop new or modified theories and models, perhaps in response to criticisms of your explicit theories and models.

Rules

There are always rules. The rules of the institution have probably not been designed primarily, if at all, to facilitate the process of development and innovation. Work with as many of them as you can; negotiate ways around those that cause particular difficulties; seek to change only those you fear will be fatal to your project. Find allies who can help with the last two processes.

NOTE AND ACKNOWLEDGEMENTS

No further contact has been made during the preparation of this chapter with the authors of the papers analysed for project management issues. Sole responsibility for the identification and discussion of project management issues lies with me as the author of the chapter. Further, no updating of the content of papers has been undertaken, although the first papers considered here were published in 1996.

I gratefully thank the authors of the papers published in the *International Journal for Academic Development* and used in this chapter; all the other *IJAD* authors; and the referees who have contributed to improving and assuring the quality of papers in the journal. I also thank my co-founding-editors of the *International Journal for Academic Development*, Dr Chris Knapper in Canada and Dr Patricia Weeks in Australia, as well as the new co-editor Dr Angela Brew, for the conversations and shared work which we hope is contributing to establishing and testing a scholarly base for our work as staff and educational developers.

REFERENCES

Baume, D and Baume, C (1996) A national scheme to develop and accredit university teachers, *International Journal for Academic Development*, **1** (2), pp 51–58

Gokcora, D (1996) Teaching assistants from the People's Republic of China and US undergraduates: perceptions of teaching and teachers, *International Journal for Academic Development*, **1** (2), pp 34–42

Grant, B and Knowles, S (2000) Flights of imagination: academic women be(com)ing writers, *International Journal for Academic Development*, **5** (1), pp 6–19

Ho, A (2000) A conceptual change approach to staff development: a model for programme design, *International Journal for Academic Development*, **5** (1), pp 30–41

Jenkins, A (1996) Discipline-based educational development, *International Journal for Academic Development*, **1** (1), pp 50–62

Johnston, S and Adams, D (1996) Trying to make a difference: experiences of establishing a new educational development unit, *International Journal for Academic Development*, **1** (1), pp 20–26

Nightingale, P (1996) Learning from experience – the teachers as well as the students, *International Journal for Academic Development*, **1** (2), pp 43–50

Schreurs, M-L, Robertson, H and Bouhuijs, A J (1999) Leading the horse to water: teacher training for all teachers in a faculty of Health Sciences, *International Journal for Academic Development*, **4** (2), pp 115–23

Smith, J and Oliver, M (2000) Academic development: a framework for embedding learning technology, *International Journal for Academic Development*, **5** (2), pp 129–37

13

Labouring 'more abundantly than they all'?

Mantz Yorke

INTRODUCTION

Until I read the preceding chapters in this book, I had not really appreciated how complex an activity project management is. I had led and managed projects, of course, but I had done this on the basis of accumulated experience (vicarious and direct) of previous projects in which I had been involved in one minor role or another. No one had codified for me a set of key issues and advice, so much of what I did owed a lot to that often hailed standby 'common sense'. And, as politicians have tended to find through experience (rather than by taking notice of philosophers), the foundations of 'common sense' are often quite shaky.

When we, the three editors, were working up the proposal for this book, we asked ourselves what the literature had to say about project management. Much of what our searches uncovered was related to industrial and commercial projects, and had little direct applicability to developmental work in higher education. We were therefore forced back on our own resources in order to move tentatively in the direction of a theoretical position. We cannot claim too much in this chapter, since theorizing about educational development project work turns out to be a much more complex matter that we had initially thought: educational development projects take place at the intersection of a number of theoretical perspectives, and the development of relevant theory requires a fuller analysis than is possible here.

POLITICAL AND EPISTEMOLOGICAL PERSPECTIVES

Educational development work implies enhancement of the educational experience in one way or another. The enhancement may be incremental (doing a task better – for example, improving the structuring of lectures) or a radical departure from current practice (doing the task in a different way, as is the case with the introduction of problem-based learning at Temasek Polytechnic in Singapore (see Chapter 11)). On occasion, the enhancement can incorporate elements of both incremental and radical change. Some time ago I saw these change possibilities in terms of an 'enhancement matrix' (shown in Figure 13.1), not realizing at the time that I had merely reinvented what Argyris (1999) had – in his earlier writings – described as 'single loop' and 'double loop' learning.

Change always takes place within a political content. The current Zeitgeist of higher education gives prominence to human capital theory (Becker, 1975), which connects the education of people to national prosperity: for two examples of evidence, see the basic presumption of the Dearing Report (NCIHE, 1997), and the introduction of the 'employment' performance indicator (HEFCE, 2001). Educational development is also inflected with a desire for social justice (see Rawls, 1999), resulting in a political desire to widen participation, and the accessibility of project outcomes has become a progressively stronger theme in successive rounds of FDTL. Educational development in higher education is unavoidably smudged with these political colourings. As a consequence, the project manager needs to keep an eye on the extent to which the sponsor's agenda is being satisfied by the project (whether the sponsor is a national body or an institution using its own money for developmental purposes).

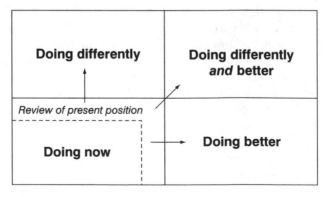

Figure 13.1   *The enhancement matrix (after Yorke, 1994)*

Project management within higher education takes place at the inter-section of a number of epistemologies, a fact that places considerable demands on the project manager (who may or may not double up in the role of project leader). Following Kotter (1990), leadership emphasizes setting a direction, motivating people and gaining their willingness to support action, whereas management is more concerned with ensuring that what is supposed to happen does actually happen: in practice, the two often overlap quite considerably. Hence the following discussion has to be interpreted and adjusted according to the reader's position.

A project manager in the field of educational development ideally needs to have the following:

- expertise in subject X (in some projects, also in Y, Z, etc);

- expertise in pedagogy, and preferably in relation to subject X (and Y, Z, etc, as appropriate);

- expertise in management; and

- a practical knowledge of organizational sociology (for example, regarding where the power lies, and how to use the knowledge to render action maximally effective).

Further, if the project manager has come into higher education after a period in another public service, in industry, or in commerce, then he or she will probably have to re-attune to the culture of higher education, but this time as experienced from the 'supply side' instead of from the perspective of a student.

There is a need here to note that circumstances vary from project to project. Most of the projects featured in this book took place within a single disciplinary culture, with the result that there was a considerable amount of tacit knowledge shared among those involved. This can be an advantage (in that there is relatively little need for the negotiation of meanings) and also a disadvantage (in that shared understandings may not be opened up to reflection and debate). In contrast to the majority, Smith's 'Sharing Excellence' project (Chapter 2) took place across a range of disciplines within a single institution, thereby inverting the advantages and disadvan-tages of the single-discipline projects. The position regarding disciplinary epistemology was, as a result, considerably more complex. Lest the 'Sharing Excellence' project be construed as an 'outlier', it should be noted that educational development promoted within institutions (perhaps as a component of an institutional learning and teaching strategy) often opens up opportunities across an institution, with someone having managerial responsibility for a slew of in-house small-scale projects.

There are few paragons who can lay claim to expertise in all of the epistemological areas listed above, and a project manager's background will determine the relative strengths that he or she brings to the job, and hence how he or she will be able to influence the project as it evolves. Smith (Chapter 2) notes the value of the project manager having expertise in the management of change.

The expertise of other people involved in the project can also be mapped against the four categories noted above. Tan, for example, reports that expertise in subject X was the dominant focus of 65 members of staff at Temasek Polytechnic, with pedagogy a long way behind (Chapter 11). Smith (Chapter 2) and Varnava (Chapter 5) note that there was, in their projects, a need to heighten academics' awareness of pedagogical matters. Broadly, there is a need for someone (typically, but not necessarily, the project manager, since it will depend on the make-up of the leading group as a whole) to blend the four kinds of expertise into a frame for thinking and action that will be accepted by the project workers as a whole. (It is probably unrealistic to expect to come up with a frame that will satisfy everyone completely: the test should perhaps be whether everyone is prepared to 'live with' what is proposed.)

THE NEED FOR 'TEAMNESS'

The improbability of omnicompetence points to the need for a project team to know who has which particular strengths. A survey of 'who is bringing what to the party' is a helpful starting point, and may well have taken place at the time when the bid for the project was being put together. What it probably will not show is how the team might work together – in other words, how roles in the team (in contrast to formal status and role) interlock. The classic work of Belbin (1981) on team roles showed how important it is for a team to be made up from people with different – and complementary – strengths: the 'Apollo Team' of highly creative people proved to be the least effective in delivering outcomes even though it was ostensibly the cleverest by a fair margin. At different times, the need is for different abilities to come to the fore – for example, creativity at one time, capacity to grind at another, and evaluating at yet another.

In my experience, I have found a complementary mix of abilities to be a significant factor in achieving outcomes with groups, with the lead being taken by different people at different times, irrespective of formal status and role. If everything is done according to hierarchical position, the outcome can be poor. I vividly recall a group of staff participating in a workshop who were faced with a problem that involved everyone pooling their information if it was to be solved. In practice, the head of department controlled things so tightly that the 'team' failed to complete what, in reality, was not a difficult task. A good leader knows when to let others have the floor, and allows others to take credit as appropriate. They are poor leaders who can do no other than cast themselves in the role of hero, commander and omnicompetent. A useful maxim is 'to go with the best idea, whoever in the team comes up with it', but this usually does not happen unless the leader takes responsibility for ensuring that it does.

ESTEEM

If educational development projects are to gain recognition by academics as worthwhile activities, then they need to key into the things that are valued in academe. Australia (see Johnstone, Chapter 10) has led the way in making a case for teaching excellence to be recognized and rewarded in a manner akin to research. Institutions in the UK have moved in this direction in recent years, with particular emphasis being given where funding councils have required institutions to produce strategies for learning and teaching, with the consequence that mechanisms for recognizing and rewarding teaching have been strengthened. However, the valuing of efforts directed towards learning and teaching remains a matter of considerable debate – and the Research Assessment Exercise (RAE) continues to exert its massive pull on staff energies, rather like a super-dense star sucking material away from a more diffuse binary companion.

Developmental projects offer research opportunities, even though they may not be constituted as research (indeed, the bidding documentation for FDTL has made it clear that the initiative has not been set up for the support of research projects). They may, as in FDTL, seek the transfer of practice around the higher education system, or they may be concerned with innovation. Either way, they open up research questions, such as 'How effective was the transfer process?' together with 'What factors encouraged or discouraged uptake?', 'Did the innovation work?', or – as Gravestock (Chapter 8) and Wisdom (Chapter 9) evidence – 'What happened as a consequence?' Questions such as these seem at first sight to be some way removed from project management, but if management involves ensuring that contributors get reward from participating, and if the dominant culture in higher education relates to research, then research-related issues are of importance to the project manager. After all, as Thomas (Chapter 7) reminds us, a developmental project can be construed as action research with a pragmatic substrate in which – and here I draw on Neurath's different sailing metaphor – we replace the rotting timbers of our ship, one by one, as it sails along, trusting the while in the structural integrity of the remainder (see Quine, 1960: 3, or Popper, 1972: 60).

However, there is a problem. Educational development projects give rise (where the opportunity is taken) to research outcomes that are almost always pedagogical in character. This means that they may not be afforded as much weight in the 'Subject X' unit of assessment in the RAE as research in Subject X itself. Although the ground rules for the 2001 RAE made it plain that pedagogic research into Subject X should be treated on a par with that in the subject itself, it is by no means clear that this in fact did happen.

Any failure to give parity of esteem to the two kinds of research (assuming comparable standards of rigour) would act as a disincentive to researching pedagogic practice within an educational development framework. One solution to the subject/pedagogy dilemma would be to treat pedagogical research in HE in a different way from subject-specific research, such that an institution's record in pedagogical research could be assessed by a panel of experts in pedagogical matters as a whole, and not in dribs and drabs in subject-specific units of assessment (see the argument in Yorke, 2000).

INPUTS, PROCESSES AND OUTPUTS

Projects can usefully be seen in terms of inputs, processes and outputs, as shown in Table 13.1. The assumption here is that a bid has already been made and approved, so for present purposes the bid documentation (including its promises) can be treated as an input.

Table 13.1 *A 'broad brush' perspective on inputs, processes and outputs*

Inputs	Processes	Outputs
Project goals and intended 'deliverables'	Keeping the project on track	Actual 'deliverables'
Timetable	Handling financial accounts	Impact
Staffing and expertise	Keeping to 'the rules', but challenging them when necessary	Collateral benefits
Resources of various kinds	Recognizing the need for flexibility, where necessary, and negotiating amendments with sponsors	
	Arranging meetings, developmental work and dissemination activities	
	Monitoring and evaluating	

To cast things thus is to risk giving a static quality to something that is highly dynamic. A project does not begin with an injection of inputs that simply go through a linear sequence of processes and, in the fullness of time, produce outputs. This approach might produce high-grade trans-former steel, but not a good educational output, since the latter depends unavoidably on an interlocking array of inputs and processes that suggests a chain mail of Kolb-like cycles of inputs, activities and reflection. However, the threefold division of Table 13.1 provides a framework for the discussion in this section.

Some project managers are in at the beginning of the development of the project proposal, even though they may not have been formally iden-tified for the role. This allows them to contribute to the project's devel-opment, and hence to shape the goals, scope, collaborative arrangements (where appropriate), resource requirements and methodologies to be used. Grant and Knowles (2000; and see Chapter 12), for example, had very clear goals for their women's writing project. Smith and Oliver (2000; and see Chapter 12) and the Geography Discipline Network's project (Chapter 8) show how the work was shaped through the engagement of putative users from the start. The more a project can work in conjunction with the intended beneficiaries, the less the likelihood that sceptics (there are almost always some, even though their scepticism may not be immediately apparent) will make life difficult. As with health, anticipation and prevention of problems are better than having to treat problems once they have erupted.

Inputs

There is not a lot to be said under this heading. A project has a budget, staffing and other resources, a specified duration and various intended outputs. When focusing on goals, there is a risk that the project team will concentrate its attention on what it has to deliver, at the expense of the broader intentions behind the project. Many – probably the vast majority of – educational development projects have as their underpinning rationale some change for the better in the student experience. Yet projects can fall into the trap of operating in 'supply side' terms, with the student voice left out of earshot: Thomas (Chapter 7), for example, acknowledges that she realized too late in the SAPHE project that it would have been better to have included students from the start. In contrast, Smallwood (Chapter 4) engaged students in the steering group for the PADSHE project.

Where the 'input' aspect of the project can experience difficulty is in the actual release of resources that were promised at the time of the bid. This can be a particular problem if promised staffing expertise fails to materialize as expected (due to factors outside the control of the project manager). Thus the wise project manager keeps a weather eye on what is supposed to happen in the near future and does not make the default assumption that what was promised will turn up. The anticipation of possible future events, however, takes the discussion into the realm of processes.

Processes

Planning and anticipating
A project usually needs to have interim targets which serve a variety of purposes. These targets constitute milestones of progress for the project team, which can be celebrated. They can act as 'encouragements' (carrot or stick variety) to contributors to deliver what they are contracted (formally or informally) to deliver. They also provide markers for sponsors against which the accountability for the use of the funds can be established. If milestones are not embodied in the project's formal plan, then it is a good idea for a project team to set these up for its own purposes. FDTL expects, as a matter of course, that projects will have a set of milestones, and this is not untypical of externally sponsored projects. This is a practice that smaller-scale internal projects could usefully emulate. After all, this is of considerable help in the monitoring of progress.

If it was not undertaken at the time of constructing the project bid, a SWOT (strengths, weaknesses, opportunities, and threats) analysis is potentially valuable. As an early contribution to team building, such an analysis can help to develop:

- a collective belief in the capacity of a project team to deliver what it has set out to do (after all, it has got the contract, so someone 'out there' believes in the project's viability);

- the confidence to accept that nothing is perfect (there is no shame in admitting this – indeed, it is a sign of maturity), and that ways of addressing weaknesses will need to be worked out;

- an open appreciation that problems (both anticipated and unanticipated) will need to be faced as the project unfolds; and, if necessary,

- a deepened conviction that the project task is worthwhile.

Many project managers have found – in some cases, to their chagrin and/or embarrassment – that the world does not organize itself around the needs of the project: people are taken ill, are required to engage on other things, or move elsewhere; records are lost in a computer crash; rooms booked for activities become unavailable at short notice; or a hotel's service for a workshop is so poor that the event organizers have, in effect, to do the hotel's job for it. Readers may be able to add their own particular horror stories to the list. Some potential problems can be anticipated and contingency plans made; others are adventitious and can only be handled as they arise. The project manager is in a pivotal position, and needs to ensure that he or she shares his or her knowledge with at least one other so that, if illness or other misfortune strikes, there is no human equivalent of a computer crash, wiping out information that has not been backed up.

The social imperative in change processes

Fullan (1991: 65) reminds us that 'Educational change is technically simple and socially complex.' This is a powerful 'one-liner' that has a lot of implications for projects and their management. 'Technically' can be construed in terms of technologically based developments (such as e-learning) or, more generally, in terms of solving a particular problem. What I take from Fullan here is that he points firmly to the necessity of dealing with the issue of getting people involved in, and committed to, change. This applies both to team members and, perhaps less immediately obviously, to those whom the project seeks to influence.

Enthusiasts for innovations and developments can sometimes find it difficult to imagine that others will be reticent about following their lead, since there is a tendency for the enthusiasts to believe that they have (or are about to obtain) solutions to problems. What they are doing is 'obviously' worthwhile, so how could any rational person not go along with them? There is something of a parallel with educational researchers who are too keen that their results should have an immediate impact on policy making (see McIntyre, 1997: 138). However, a sceptical stance on the part of those who have seen innovations come and go is reasonable: they may have doubts about the problem that the development is seeking to solve, the benefit/cost ratio of the development (even if it delivers what it sets out to do), or about the willingness of colleagues to change existing practices.

I will illustrate the need to engage potential users of a project's outputs by drawing on my experience with the 'Skills Plus' project which is funded by HEFCE (though not under FDTL auspices), and has involved 16 departments in four varied universities in the north-west of England.[1] In short, this project seeks to establish an alignment between 'employability' and good learning, and to capture this by tweaking (rather than by radically reconstructing) curricula – a 'low pain, high gain' approach. The project has the advantage of a theoretical position that is based on research: this is not a typical feature of educational development projects, many of which are driven from a discipline other than education. It may be worthwhile for future educational development projects to identify a theoretical grounding in an educationally relevant discipline if they are to maximize the 'street cred' of their processes and outputs in the eyes of their academic colleagues. However, it must be acknowledged that education is not always seen as a high status discipline, and so the benefits of adopting this approach may not be as forthcoming as they ought.

The 'Skills Plus' project's possession of a theoretical base has shown itself to be intrinsically attractive to academics who are suspicious of narrowly conceived 'key skills' interventions. Further, the project has also not sought to overturn existing practices, on the grounds that going with the prevailing grain is more likely to lead to success than cutting across it.[2] Above all, the project has worked in conjunction with those it has sought to influence: for example, it has run, throughout its duration, a series of colloquia at which papers and reports of work carried out in participant departments have been brought together and discussed. In other words, the project has addressed the social imperative of Fullan's words.

Knowing how the institutional finance system works

For processes to work optimally, the project manager needs to know how the institutions involved operate. At the simplest technical level, a knowledge of the way in which the budget-holding institution's finance system works is essential. Some institutional procedures are more transparent than others, and some finance personnel are more helpful than others. There is also a need to know what the written and unwritten rules of relevant institutions are. A project manager appointed from within an institution has an advantage, and an outsider is faced with climbing a steep learning curve, in a fog of uncertainty as to where the key information is to be found. The guidance of those who know the ropes is likely to prove invaluable, especially when the project manager is thrown in at the deep end right away, as Thomas (Chapter 7) was, and has to come up with some quick achievements.

Varnava (Chapter 5), in discussing the broader issue of managing resources, gives some useful hints regarding the management of a project budget. After all, the project manager needs to know where the money is going, and what remains available for use.

Political awareness

This is 'political-with-a-small-p' awareness. Knowing who wants what from the project, knowing where support is likely to be found (and where the opposite might be the case), and an appreciation of the institutional (and/or departmental) culture are insights that can make one's life as a project manager easier. As Thomas (Chapter 7) observes, drawing on Carr and Kemmis (1986), an understanding of context is important in appreciating where an educational development is likely to be successful.

Political awareness contributes to an understanding of the formal and informal rules adopted by an institution. Occasionally, there is tension between what the project seeks to achieve and the way that the institution goes about its business. It may be possible to make a change to the rules, and here the support of senior people may facilitate the necessary changes. An alternative is to be creative in dealing with the rules: there may be a way of finessing the situation such that the rules are being complied with, but in a novel and imaginative way.

Using a steering group

Smallwood (Chapter 4) has stressed the value that can accrue from a steering group. A steering group is, however, often seen in rather limited terms – perhaps merely as a body to which reports have to be provided, and from which approval for some actions has to be sought. A well-constituted steering group can be much more useful than that, since the expertise of its members can be brought productively to bear on the project's work. It may be able to add its weight to the work of the project team, providing the 'clout' to ensure that the team's voice is heard in the right quarters. Hence the establishment of a steering group needs to be undertaken with a view to what its members might be able to add to the project's work. This involves another dimension of political awareness.

Group dynamics

The group dynamics of a project team are important. The project manager is often in a position to exercise leadership, even if he or she is – in status terms – a relatively lowly part of the team. With the (possible) exception of the project director, the project manager may be the person most able to see the project as a whole and appreciate what is going well and what may not be working as it was intended, and envisage what is possible and not possible. The project manager is likely to write the minutes of meetings, and probably will have considerable influence over the setting of agendas. If knowledge is power, then the project manager might have more power than he or she realizes. As politics often evidences, a person a pace or two behind the apparent leader may be the one who exercises the real power.

The project manager is in a position to keep a watchful eye on the extent to which team members are engaged. If not combining the role with that of project leader, he or she can – indeed, should – keep the leader au fait with who is (and is not) doing what. This should enable the leader to take steps to ensure that each team member is contributing appropriately to the collective good.

Most people have a need to be credited with their engagement with 'their' project, and one of the early necessities is to agree a general way in which this is to be done. If this is left until the end, then there can be unseemly wrangles about who should be credited for what. There is also an ongoing need to ensure that outcomes are celebrated as they happen, and are not taken for granted. This is all part of keeping colleagues 'on-side' with regard to the project.

The need for flexibility

The more complex the design of the project, the greater the chances that something untoward will happen. Different disciplinary cultures might affect a cross-disciplinary project, as Smith (Chapter 2) found. Smith's solution, in the vernacular, was to 'go with the flow', and not to let the project's original ideal of standardization attempt to override the disciplinary culture, on the grounds that standardization could have had adverse consequences. This is the kind of issue with which managers of cross-disciplinary development projects are likely to have to grapple.

More broadly, the 'project on paper' may have to be modified in the light of events. There is a need for flexibility and adaptability when dealing with institutional turbulence and other contingencies, as June Balshaw's experience with the TALESSI Project (Chapter 6) has shown. The corollary is that any significant amendment needs to be justified to (or, indeed, negotiated with) sponsors – and the sooner the better. The relationship with the sponsor should be one of partnership – after all, both the sponsor and the project team are seeking to bring about an agreed change. It is not politic to present a sponsor with a fait accompli.

Efficiency and effectiveness

If a project delivers exactly what it promised, then this can be represented as an efficient use of resources. A narrow focus on the letter of the project contract may, however, distract attention from the spirit of what was agreed. If an opportunity arises to exploit an unanticipated possibility without significant disruption to what is planned, then it surely makes sense to grab it rather than let it pass. It would cost (probably considerably) more to have to deal with it as a new, free-standing issue. However, doing something orig-inally unplanned implies omitting something that was planned. Limitations on time and resources make for a zero-sum game.

Maximizing efficiency (with respect to the original plan) may lead to sub-optimal effectiveness. Some slack (in the sense of things that can be traded off) may prove to be advantageous over the longer term. As a loose analogy, the tribulations of the National Health Service show that running hospitals at full bed occupancy can militate against coping with epidemics, for example. The world is rarely as tidily organized as planners would wish.

Networking

Networking is valuable in a number of respects. Fincher (Chapter 3) draws attention to the different kinds of networks: the 'noun based' and the 'verb based'. These are primarily concerned, in different ways, with getting the task done. However, networking has other, less immediately tangible, uses.

Being in a network opens up the possibility of finding out what else is going on in the area of the project, with the possibility that this will stimulate new thinking or help in the finding of solutions to problems. The National Co-ordination Team (NCT) has provided projects in later rounds of FDTL, and in other programmatic project areas, with activities designed to achieve these two purposes. These activities can help project leaders to engage in virtual contact as well as more direct, face-to face meetings. The value of such groupings as support groups should not be overlooked. The role of project manager, in some circumstances, can be very isolated, and the support of people in similar positions can help with difficulties of different kinds. Johnston and Adams (1996: see Chapter 12) hint at the value that can be gained from engaging with peers in similar situations.

Towards the beginning of this chapter, mention was made of the complexity that underlies the role of the manager of an educational devel-opment project. A network of project managers comes close to what Wenger (1998) would term a 'community of practice', and offers the prospect of assisting a project manager to develop an understanding of the role, and to enact it more effectively than might otherwise be the case.

Outputs, outcomes and impact

First, a clarification of terms, as used here:

- **Outputs**: these are the intended 'deliverables' – the things that the project was funded to provide.

- **Outcomes**: this is a broader term, which subsumes the range of things that happened as a consequence of the project, both planned and unplanned (in Table 13.1, these are the 'deliverables' and the collateral benefits).

- **Impact**: this is an assessment of the amount of influence the outcomes actually had.

The three terms manifestly overlap.

Bids for later rounds of FDTL have placed a lot of emphasis on the production of Web sites, newsletters and the like. There is a danger, however, that making information available is construed as making an impact. However, while those who need to know about the project and its outcomes will undoubtedly make the effort to seek out the relevant information, those who lack an immediate 'need to know' will probably not follow up the leads, probably because other things have a greater pull on their attention. Making information available is a 'supply side' matter – necessary but not sufficient, as far as impact goes.

In his chapter on dissemination, Gravestock (Chapter 8) takes a 'demand side' perspective, describing how attempts were made to determine the impact of the geography project on practice through the use of telephone interviews some months after a workshop had taken place. Wisdom, in discussing evaluation (Chapter 9), indicates that he noticed qualitative changes in the way in which those involved in History 2000 interacted, and the emergence of a shared language. These kinds of evaluative activity can never be an exact science, but are likely to provide evidence of impact that is rather stronger than apparently 'harder' quantitative data such as the numbers attending workshops, counts of hits on Web sites, and scores on satisfaction questionnaires.

SUSTAINABILITY

Increasingly, proposers of projects are asked how their work will continue to be effective once the specific funding has run out. They have to come up with a continuation strategy. The embedding of developed practice has long been a problem: many are the projects whose dynamism waned with the ending of the budget. It is not surprising, therefore, that funders are increasingly looking for projects that offer a reasonable prospect of sustainability. The key to sustainability is engagement. Two necessary conditions for sustainability are (1) the commitment of colleagues to the project, and (2) the presence of an infrastructure that actively promotes the outputs of the project with those who have hitherto not been involved.

The first condition can, as was noted earlier, be met through the project methodology (which has to be designed to engender a sense of ownership). The second is more difficult. By and large, projects do not have the resources to extend their work beyond the budgeted period. Some may have the advantage of being connected to organizations that can, in one way or another, keep some momentum going. However, a commitment for the longer term may not be forthcoming from such organizations, for various understandable reasons. With the advent of the Learning and Teaching Support Network (in particular) in the UK, the second condition can be met provided that the Generic Centre and/or the 24 Subject Centres engage with the project and act to broker the take-up of what it has to offer. For FDTL Phase Four the expectation – indeed, the requirement – is that projects will liaise with the appropriate part of the LTSN in order to enhance dissemination both during and beyond the period of funding. For in-house projects, the primary issue is likely to be transfer and uptake in departments other than that (or those) in which the project was implemented, since a 'within department' project has by its nature a reasonable prospect of continuation beyond the period of funding.

COMMUNICATION

The Economic and Social Research Council has, in its Teaching and Learning Research Programme, made a point of stressing the communication of research outcomes – not only at the end of the various funded projects, but also as they unfold. The intention is clear: to stimulate engagement and hence to increase the chances that findings will be applied. A similar determination that projects should not be 'closed off' has come to pervade initiatives such as FDTL, and the establishment of the Learning and Teaching Support Network has increased the possibility that project outcomes will be spread throughout the higher education system.

Communication needs to be considered in terms of flow both inwards and outwards. Inward communication involves the contribution of potential users (staff, students and – perhaps – others, such as professional bodies) to the development of the project deliverables. The deliverables will have been envisaged at the time of constructing the project bid, but possibly in general terms rather than in specific detail. As the project develops, opportunities will almost certainly exist to engage the intended users in refining the intended outcomes and in contributing to their development.

Communication from the project has three main dimensions:

- keeping project team members and associates 'in the loop';
- informing sponsors of progress and of any significant difficulties that have been encountered; and
- conveying project outcomes to 'the outside world'.

The first point is self-evident. Where a project spans institutions, or disciplines within an institution, the need is for all who are involved to know what is going on, and how their part fits into the broader whole. Whereas a small group within, say, a department may be able handle this on a relatively informal basis, more complex patterns of engagement require more formalized methods of communication. Electronic communication has the virtues of speed and directness, and offers the possibility of quick response. Newsletters can be made to look attractive, but the danger is that they will be filed for later reading and gradually become overlain with strata of more recently arrived paperwork. However, these methods tend to be 'centre to periphery' modes of communication. If a project is to be a properly shared experience, then consideration has to be given to arranging events that bring people together in order to engage with substantive issues. Where distance and travel create problems, then teleconferencing may serve as a substitute for direct face-to-face conversation.

Projects sponsored by national bodies are subject to the bodies' reporting arrangements. Thus projects sponsored under the FDTL (and other projects under the wing of the Higher Education Funding Council for England) are required to report on a quarterly basis to the National Co-ordination Team, whose brief is not only to gather in reports but also to support projects in various ways and to arrange events that are designed to share what has been learnt from projects with the higher education system as a whole. If a project runs into severe difficulties, then the NCT may need to advise the sponsor regarding the continuation of funding.

Projects run within institutions are subject to the institutions' reporting requirements. Ideally, there should be a process through which the learning from various in-house projects is brought together for the purposes of sharing both what has been learnt about the projects' achievements, and what has been learnt about the practicalities of running the projects. Sadly, such a process does not always exist.

Most projects seek to have an influence that extends beyond the 'home' department(s), and hence communication to others is a significant consideration. Often there is potential for holding events based on interim outputs. Events of this sort act to flag up not only the fact that the project is under way, but also that it might have value for those beyond the project itself. They may well cause a beneficial influx of new ideas. They also have the virtue of helping the project team take stock of where it is, collectively to celebrate its achievements to date, and – perhaps – to enjoy positive feedback on what it has done so far. Such an activity not only puts the project on the map, it also helps in the development of the team as a team. Interim outcomes as process, perhaps.

It is again self-evident that the main project deliverables have to be communicated as widely as intended. At the time of FDTL Phase One, there was no LTSN to provide disciplinary conduits for the sharing either of artefacts of varying kinds, or of other developed expertise. Nowadays in the UK there is a more strategic approach to applications deriving from projects, and this is replicated within institutions where learning and teaching strategies give a focus to developments that, in yesteryear, would probably have been achieved in relative isolation.

CONCLUSION

This book has shown how complex and demanding is the role of the manager of an educational development project. The preceding chapters have brought to life, in a way that a more technical text cannot do, the trials, tribulations and successes of those who have managed in a number of project contexts. For greater detail regarding the tasks of the project manager, and for a complementary technical perspective, the manual published by the NCT (undated) is likely to prove an invaluable source of information.

The project manager has to engage with at least three different discourses – the subject, education and management – and perhaps a fourth, organizational sociology. If the project manager is responsible for projects in a number of disciplines, then he or she has to come to terms with the concomitant multiplicity of subject-specific discourses. Engaging with a range of discourses is, of course, a necessary but insufficient condition for the fulfilment of the project manager's role, for fulfilment demands the exercise of a range of operational skills if the project is to be brought to fruition.

I hope that project managers who read this book will find various insights that will help them to do well the job to which they were appointed. As I draw this book to a close, another thought strikes me: how many managers of project managers appreciate the complexity of the latter's role? Maybe, when they have read this text, project managers ought to leave their copy quietly on their manager's desk. Such a gentle display of 'managing upwards' might prove rewarding.

NOTES

1 For a number of papers relating to this project, see http://www.open.ac.uk/
   vqportal/Skills-Plus/home.htm.
2 This has not precluded one department going further, and using the project as a
   stimulus to the development of a curriculum centring on problem-based
   learning.

REFERENCES

Argyris, C (1999) *On Organizational Learning*, 2nd edn, Blackwell, Oxford
Becker, G S (1975) *Human Capital*, Chicago University Press, Chicago
Belbin, M (1981) *Management Teams: Why they succeed or fail*, Butterworth-
   Heinemann, Oxford
Carr, W and Kemmis, S (1986) *Becoming Critical: Education, knowledge and action
   research*, Falmer, London
Fullan, M (1991) *The New Meaning of Educational Change*, Cassell, London
Grant, B and Knowles, S (2000) Flights of imagination: academic women
   be(com)ing writers, *International Journal for Academic Development*, **5** (1), pp 6–19
Higher Education Funding Council for England (HEFCE) (2001) *Indicators of
   Employment* (01/21), HEFCE, Bristol
Johnston, S and Adams, D (1996) Trying to make a difference: experiences of estab-
   lishing a new educational development unit, *International Journal for Academic
   Development*, **1** (1), pp 20–26
Kotter, J (1990) *A Force for Change: How leadership differs from management*, Free Press,
   New York
McIntyre, D (1997) The profession of educational research, *British Educational
   Research Journal*, **23** (2), pp 127–40
NCIHE (1997) *Higher Education in the Learning Society* (report of the National
   Committee of Inquiry into Higher Education), HMSO, London
National Coordination Team (NCT) (undated) *Project Manager's Handbook*, NCT,
   Open University, Milton Keynes
Popper, K R (1972) *Objective Knowledge*, Oxford University Press, Oxford
Quine, W van O (1960) *Word and Object*, MIT Press, Cambridge, Mass
Rawls, J (1999) *A Theory of Justice*, new edn, Oxford University Press, Oxford
Smith, J and Oliver, M (2000) UK academic development: a framework for
   learning technology, *International Journal for Academic Development*, **5** (2),
   pp 129–37
Wenger, E (1998) *Communities of Practice: Learning, meaning and identity*, Cambridge
   University Press, Cambridge
Yorke, M (1994) Enhancement-led higher education? *Quality Assurance in Education*,
   2 (3), pp 6–12
Yorke, M (2000) A cloistered virtue? Pedagogical research and policy in UK higher
   education, *Higher Education Quarterly*, **54** (2), pp 106–26

ACKNOWLEDGEMENT

My thanks to Jon Yorke for reminding me of the Fullan quotation.

Index